LILLIAN TOO
JENNIFER TOO

FORTUNE & FENG SHUI

DOG 2015

in the year of the wood sheep

KONSEPBOOKS
ASTROLOGY . FENG SHUI . INSPIRATIONS

My Dear Readers,

The good news for the coming Sheep Year is that the chart is well-balanced. It is also not as fierce as the previous year. The Sheep is a docile sign, more comfortable with diplomacy than with any show of force or anger. The main problem is that at the mankind level, the feng shui chart indicates the hostility star dominating, so there will continue to be mistrust and misunderstanding. Nevertheless, the energies of the year are very favourable for business expansion and commerce.

Relationship luck can be difficult and couples go through some rough periods. Timing is thus crucial when it comes to making and executing decisions. So as you enter into the New Year, remind yourself to...

Live in a state of greater awareness
so that opportunities do not pass you by.

****

Make a special effort to be patient with loved ones to counter hostility vibes. The best remedy for the year's hostility vibes are the Allies & Friends Crests.

****

Watch your health and put all your remedies in place.

****

Enhance your personal Windhorse for success.

This edition of Fortune & Feng Shui 2015 walks you through the most important points to take note of through the year. It also directly analyses your personalized horoscope charts for the coming year based on your animal sign. This enables you to check your lucky and unlucky months, and to navigate through the year in a way that opens your eyes to big opportunities. This gives you a real edge in business, competitive sports or career situations. Many have found our Fortune & Feng Shui annual books invaluable for helping them make wise and timely decisions in relation to their travel, career, relationships and business.

This little book contains a wealth of condensed information pertinent to your animal sign as we explain in detail the different astrological and feng shui forces influencing your sign. It alerts you to what you can expect and how you can stay protected, while expanding auspicious indications in the different areas of your life in 2015.

Discover the wonderful benefits of Feng Shui that go hand in hand with the information that has been painstakingly incorporated into this little book. Yes, there is a wealth of information inside that is easy to understand and practical to use!

Meanwhile, can I invite you to join my FENG SHUI "MANDALA". By subscribing to my fortnightly EZINE newsletter, I will send you updates on time dimension feng shui, bring you anecdotes to amuse and amaze you, and share some wonderful spiritual feng shui experiences with you. The EZINE will also bring you plenty of tips that address the three dimensions of feng shui - space, time and spiritual. I shall also be releasing a brand new book this coming year, as well as the MOST beautiful feng shui products that are sure to catch your fancy and bring you lots of luck. Much of this and other information will be part of the newsletter, so do register and enjoy.

Our newsletter is FREE and it is easy to register. Just go to *www.wofs.com* and sign in!

BIG HUG for a great Year of the Sheep!

Lillian

Fortune & Feng Shui 2015 Dog
by Lillian Too and Jennifer Too
© 2015 Konsep Lagenda Sdn Bhd

Text © 2015 Lillian Too and Jennifer Too
Photographs and illustrations © WOFS.com Sdn Bhd

The moral right of the authors to be identified as authors of this book has
been asserted.

Published by KONSEP LAGENDA SDN BHD (223 855)
Kuala Lumpur 59100 Malaysia

For more Konsep books, go to www.lillian-too.com or www.wofs.com
To report errors, please send a note to errors@konsepbooks.com
For general feedback, email feedback@konsepbooks.com

ISBN 978-967-329-153-3
Published in Malaysia, August 2014

DOG 2015

BIRTH YEAR	WESTERN CALENDAR DATES	AGE	KUA NUMBER MALES	KUA NUMBER FEMALES
FIRE Dog	2 Feb 1946 to 21 Jan 1947	69	9 East Group	6 West Group
EARTH Dog	18 Feb 1958 to 7 Feb 1959	57	6 West Group	9 East Group
METAL Dog	6 Feb 1970 to 26 Jan 1971	45	3 East Group	3 East Group
WATER Dog	25 Jan 1982 to 12 Feb 1983	33	9 East Group	6 West Group
WOOD Dog	10 Feb 1994 to 30 Jan 1995	21	6 West Group	9 East Group
FIRE Dog	29 Jan 2006 to 17 Feb 2007	9	3 East Group	3 East Group

DOG 2015

The Dog in 2015 is feeling romantic and tends to be touchy-feely this year, extra affectionate and ever eager to see the nicest side to every situation. This loyal and dependable sign that is probably one of the nicest personalities of the Zodiac comes under the influence of the Peach Blossom, so love and passion intermingle easily in a heady mix of intoxication.

The Dog sign is already everybody's best friend, and amongst the Chinese Zodiac signs is easily the most physically demonstrative and generous. You show enormous courage when fighting for principles dear to your heart; and you are a big mama type person when it comes to looking after those placed under your care. The male Dog is similarly kind-hearted, so yours is a sign never lacking for friends. The Dog wins easily in any popularity contest and should you be involved in social work, you will actually be quite a star.

But you can be naïve when it comes to playing the political game. In the coming months of 2015, you could find success in many endeavours hard to come by; and victory can be quite elusive. Still, the Dog sign is unlikely to lose its good nature and happy disposition.

The outstanding thing usually associated with the Dog sign is your outstanding loyalty to those close to you. The Dog rarely gives up on friends and family, who can often be the cause of various kinds of aggravations in your life. In the long run however, you are rewarded beyond your wildest dreams, as those you have helped along the way come back into your life bearing gifts and friendships that prove significant to you at the time that they re-enter your lives. In Chinese, we call this the goodwill factor (karm cheng) and the Dog sign has this in droves.

The Dog male or female is tolerant and contented, being neither madly materialistic nor overly ambitious. You justifiably enjoy the limelight and appreciation that come your way, and you love socializing and flirting every now and again, but you possess conventional wisdom in good measure.

In 2015, it is a good idea to enjoy others showering love and care over you. This is a good year to enjoy the harvesting of goodwill generated through the years.

CONTENTS

CHAPTER 1.
LUCK OF THE DOG IN 2015
Good fortune indications in relationships & in your work

12

- Element Luck of the Dog 2015   19
- Dog's Wealth Luck in 2015   19
- Dog's Health Luck in 2015   22
- Life Force & Spirit Essence   24
- Dog's Love Luck in 2015   26
- Dog's Work Luck in 2015   27
- Dog's Business Luck in 2015   28

CHAPTER 2.
SHEEP YEAR 2015
A Well-Balanced Year

29

- Luck of the Wood Sheep Year 2015   30
- Luck of the Ally Groupings   40
- Paht Chee Chart of 2015   53
- Flying Star Chart of 2015   70
- The Numbers 1 to 9   73
- 2015 Feng Shui Chart is ruled by the Number 3 76
- Star of Romance in the Northwest   86
- Safeguarding the West   88

- Three Killings in the West 92
- Suppressing the Illness Star 2 in the Southeast 94
- Cure for the Dangerous 7 in the South 97
- Star of Future Prosperity in the Southwest 100
- Star of 6 in the Northeast 104
- Energizing 8 in the North 105
- Energizing 1 in the East 109

CHAPTER 3.
24 MOUNTAINS & THE HO TUS OF 2015

- 24 Mountains Stars of 2015 112
- North & South - Big Auspicious Luck All Round 115
- Southeast - A Trio of Good Fortune 118
- Northwest - Benefitting from the Earth Seal 121
- West - Very afflicted in 2015 124
- East - Facing the Three Killings 127
- Southwest - Benefits from Tai Sui 128
- Northeast - Benefitting from Heaven Luck 130
- HO TU Combinations 2015 132
- The HO TU Square & Its Number Combinations 136
- The 2/7 Combination in the Sounteast 138
- The 3/8 Combination in the Center 139
- The 4/9 Combination in the Northwest 139
- The 1/6 Combination in the East 140
- HO TU Mirrors for 2015 140

CHAPTER 4.
THE DOG'S LOVE LIFE IN 2015
Unwilling to engage emotionally even though there are opportunities to do so... 146

- Compatibility with Each Animal Sign 147
- Activating Marriage Luck 162
- **Dog & Rat** - Not living up to expectations 165
- **Dog & Ox** - A passionate time for these Earth signs 167
- **Dog & Tiger** - An excellent time for a fabulous pair 169
- **Dog & Rabbit** - Loved up pair leans in on Rabbit's strength 171
- **Dog & Dragon** - Incompatibility gets stretched 173
- **Dog & Snake** - Dog woos Snake, but with little success 175
- **Dog & Horse** - Allies make for an endearing pair 177
- **Dog & Sheep** - Love seems to waft sweet fragrance 179
- **Dog & Monkey** - Resilience of the Dog benefits the pairing 181
- **Dog & Rooster** - Strong match overcoming obstacles 183
- **Dog & Dog** - Resentment clouds an otherwise happy relationship 185
- **Dog & Boar** - A challenging time for this pair 187

CHAPTER 5.
ANALYSING YOUR LUCK IN EACH MONTH
Redefining happiness and finding contentment in other areas of life... 189

Feb 2015 - Sum-of-ten indicates a very auspicious start to the year 190

Mar 2015 - Misfortune star slows you down 193

April 2015 - Relationships take centerstage this month 196

May 2015 - Quarrelsome time with an excess of wood energy 199

June 2015 - Illness star saps you of energy 202

July 2015 - Victory star brings promise of competitive success 205

Aug 2015 - Doubling of the HO TU , brings great benefits! 208

Sept 2015 - Current prosperity star brings more lucky indications
your way 211

Oct 2015 - Afflicted energies this month. Risk of loss, betrayal. 214

Nov 2015 - Heaven star brings new opportunities & success luck 217

Dec 2015 - Misfortune star manifests temporary obstacles
to hurdle 220

Jan 2016 - Double peach blossom. Fires up the romance! 223

CHAPTER 1
LUCK OF THE DOG IN 2015
General Prospects for the Year

LUCK OF THE DOG IN 2015
GOOD FORTUNE INDICATIONS IN RELATIONSHIPS & IN YOUR WORK

The Dog enters 2015 in a happy and very relaxed state of mind. This sign can manifest indecision and ambivalence through most of the year, and this basically reflects a lack of inner confidence and self-assurance. But because the Dog is usually very humble and understated, this will not be too obvious.

The good news is that your ambivalence arises from your own higher expectations of yourself. Appearance-wise you will continue to be your normal self. Happily also, this in no way reflects what's ahead for you this year. It only reflects the way you regard yourself based on your element horoscope. But in terms of luck, the feng shui chart of the year is indicating a great deal of good fortune in your relationship luck, and there is also excellent business luck coming your way this year.

The Dog can expect to see the blossoming of happiness occasions this year. Some big issue which had been bothering you previously should work itself out – not necessarily in a very happy way, but nevertheless, at least there will be a resolution, making

13

life a lot easier and happier. There will continue to be good news on the work side of your life, so when you look back on the year, you will feel gratified that many things actually worked out better than you expected.

> ## It is that kind of year where good fortune is not immediately obvious and you can only realize it as good fortune when you look back with the benefit of hindsight.

The Dog has enjoyed some intensive highs and lows in the past years. Last year was a relatively challenging year in terms of other people's expectations of you, but it was also a highly satisfying year in terms of results and actual wealth creation. This year, loved ones and family will once again bring you equal amounts of happiness and heartache, but as always, the Dog sign copes and moves on.

The perceptions of the Dog parent this year will be more emotional than ever. The Dog is very big on family togetherness and harmony, and for many of you, this aspect of life takes higher precedence in your scale of considerations than other matters. Those of you Dogs who may be in a high profile careers may develop serious doubts about carrying on your current lifestyle. It is to this category of the sign that ambivalence becomes a big issue.

Those of you tiring of the high expectations lifestyle may decide to make some life-changing decisions, and the catalyst making you think seriously about taking this route would be the powerful *Peach Blossom* influence that is affecting you. The **33 year old Water Dog** could be in such a situation, and if so, do consider carefully before doing anything drastic.

The **45 year old Metal Dog** has romantic entanglements to contend with, but for you, this is a year when your wealth creation luck is at an all-time high. Nevertheless, you will find yourself being mentally disturbed by an unexpected attraction to someone. Hence the ambivalence you will be feeling this year. Again, the advice here is to follow conventional wisdom in such matters. Love oftentimes cause more problems than one realizes at the time it happens. As for the **57 year old Earth Dog**, if you are confronted with this sort of uncertainty, for you it is far better to walk away from temptation.

The Dog sits on the afflicted *Star of Yearly Killings* brought by the 24 Mountains, which means that there will be at least one traumatic event that could cause you to feel unsettled this year. The *Yearly Killings Star* meanwhile could make you feel a little disoriented; it requires you to be internally strong, which unfortunately is difficult for you because this year, your spirit essence is also weak. Next to this star on the Dog's left is the *Star of Yin House*, once again not a good indication; and on your right in the W3 location is the *Star of Three Killings*.

For the Dog then, we suggest you focus on creating as much Yang Chi around you as possible. This means surrounding yourself with friends, people, music, sounds, activity and plenty of bright light. The creation of yang energy will help you feel strong and revitalized; and since your intrinsic energy is Earth, it will be very beneficial to enhance your aura with Fire element energy.

It is not a good idea to stay out too late at nights and do extend this warning also to those of your loved ones whom you hold dear. The afflictions of the 24 Mountains affect not just you but also those near and dear to you.

This year, the Wood Sheep will open up a mountain of treasures for all to savour and enjoy. The Dog should therefore be alert to opportunities to make sure you are "in the loop" so to speak. This will ensure you do not lose out when it comes to opportunities becoming available. There are good reasons to adopt a strongly optimistic attitude, even if you may not be feeling confident. This is because the Dog will end the year feeling stronger and much happier. You will look back on 2015 and realize that good fortune is often preceded by challenging situations.

> The main thing that stands in the way of the Dog is that your *lung ta*, your personal Windhorse is at a very bad level this year. It is as weak as it can be. Your spirit essence is also not at a good level, so there is a lack of good cosmic winds. Your Windhorse cannot fly high.

When your *lung ta* is weak, success luck gets blocked and cannot manifest. You are better off accepting this and take a longer term view to whatever it is you are doing or have planned for completion this year. Nevertheless, you should try to strengthen your *lung ta* with element remedies, especially if you have the chance to do so.

Strengthening your *lung ta* is not difficult, as all you need to do is participate in the cosmic rituals associated with raising the Windhorse. This dissolves the obstacles to your success luck. For the Dog, it is definitely beneficial to enhance your *lung ta* in 2015 by raising the flag of the Windhorse. Hang specially-printed flags that have the Windhorse image and its four celestial guardians high up in the house or take part releasing the flags into the skies from a high mountain. This will energize your personal Windhorse!

Sending the Windhorse into the skies has been a popular ritual amongst the mountain people of China and Tibet. This involves sending as many Windhorse images, its four protector guardians and its mantras as high into the skies as possible.

These days this ritual can be done off the top of skyscrapers or from hilltops using helium-filled balloons, but this is not as effective as going to a real mountain and releasing literally thousands of pre-printed flags into the great blue skies!

For the Dog, it is definitely beneficial to raise the Windhorse during the month of the Lunar New Year or during the Spring season at the start of the year. This ritual is best done as a group, although it can also be done alone.

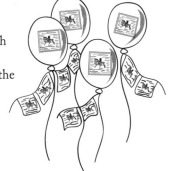

ELEMENT LUCK
OF THE DOG IN 2015

Overleaf is the Element Luck Chart for the Dog in 2015. Examine it and you will see your element luck this year looks quite challenging. There is not much in terms of *strong* or *excellent* indications; there are instead some *bad* indications for the Dog so you are definitely in need of assurances in 2015. But at least your Life Force luck is good even though your Spirit Essence luck is bad.

These two categories represent the strength of your physical and mental self. The Spirit Essence is your inner chi and with it at a negative level means you get stressed out easily and you are sensitive to criticism and arrogance. Physically however, you are fine; it is only the mental and inner state that can be of some concern. In any case, you will worry a great deal in 2015 whether or not you really need to be worried! The Dog has a good Life Force this year, but is weak in the Spirit Essence category.

WEALTH LUCK IN 2015

In the category of Wealth Luck, the **45 year old Metal Dog** and the **69 year old Fire Dog** enjoy an abundant year filled with stable income streams and a likelihood of windfall luck. For these two Dogs, this year is a

ELEMENT LUCK

2015	FIRE DOG 69/9 years	EARTH DOG 57 years
LIFE FORCE	GOOD O	GOOD O
HEALTH	NEUTRAL OX	VERY BAD XX
WEALTH	EXCELLENT OOO	VERY GOOD OO
SUCCESS WIND HORSE	VERY BAD XX	VERY BAD XX
SPIRIT ESSENCE	BAD X	BAD X

The indications of the five aspects of luck affecting the prospects for Dogs in 2015 are summarized in this table.

of the DOG IN 2015

METAL DOG *45 years*	WATER DOG *33 years*	WOOD DOG *21 years*	YEAR ELEMENT
GOOD O	GOOD O	GOOD O	EARTH
BAD X	EXCELLENT OOO	VERY GOOD OO	METAL
VERY GOOD OO	NEUTRAL OX	BAD X	WOOD
VERY BAD XX	VERY BAD XX	VERY BAD XX	FIRE
BAD X	BAD X	BAD X	FIRE

good time to focus on wealth-enhancing activities. For those of you in business, this is not a good time to retire as you can add much to the wealth-generating chi of your company.

The **57 year old Earth Dog** must be careful about finances. For you, there can be financial instability, bringing some difficulty this year. Watch your expenditure and be discerning when trusting others. Enhance your financial well-being by increasing Metal around you. **Wearing gold** is effective for maintaining financial stability.

HEALTH LUCK IN 2015

In terms of health luck, the **33 year old Water Dog** and **21 year old Wood Dog** enjoy excellent readings. But **45 year old Metal Dog** and **57 year old Earth Dog** could have to endure health-related issues.

Both these Dogs must be extra mindful of weather changes and flu bugs that cause you to lose your voice or have throat problems. Watch your personal hygiene and watch what you eat. Getting sick can be difficult for the Dog sign, as you are not the kind of person who enjoys staying in bed!

If you look at the 24 Mountains chart in another section of this book, you will find that the Northwest 1 sector - your sign's home location - plays host to the *Yearly Killings Star* this year; on your right is the *Sitting Three Killings* (in West 3) and on the left is *Star of Yin House*. All three stars brought your way by the 24 Mountains in 2015 are afflictive.

You will need to address these issues as these stars bring yin energies to you and those around you. You need to combat this excess of yin by increasing yang chi energy around you.

The Dog must neutralize the impact of the *Three Killings Star* by placing the **Three Celestial Guardians** in the West 3 location of whichever room you spend time in. Usually this should be sufficient. But you can also try facing West 3 directly should you sit facing this direction.

Everyone needs to subdue the afflictive stars of the 24 Mountains that threaten their wellbeing each year. This helps to balance the frequencies of space around you. It is vital to know the remedy needed to override conflict stars to harmonize the frequencies of your surrounding space. This is part of spatial cleansing associated with ensuring good feng shui. Once you get into the habit of updating your feng shui each New Year, tuning into the frequencies of your space should become second nature!

> For the Dog, your frequency this year is conducive to you being more relaxed. Do not get overly discouraged because your success luck frequency is weak. Remember that there are ways to remedy most negative indications, and this is the reason it is so useful to have at least remedial knowledge about astrology and feng shui.

LIFE FORCE & SPIRIT ESSENCE IN 2015

Your **Life Force** reflects the strength of your body and your mind. Your Life Force is good so you will not be feeling weak. This should give you the confidence to move steadily forward. Depend on your own strength, stay positive but also be mindful of good advice when it is sent your way. Your **Spirit Essence** however is showing a bad reading this year, so your nerves are irritated and you are feeling ambivalent. You are plagued by self-doubt, and your attitude is defeatist. This year, let go of your instincts, seek out wise counsel and think before acting. The best thing about having a weak spirit essence is that you will be more careful about taking the easy route when it comes to making difficult decisions. Also you will be more mindful when dark energies are sent your way. **Wear amulets and powerful protection** so you do not fall victim to harmful magic wheels or become vulnerable to gossip or backbiting. When the spirit is strong, it creates its own inbuilt amulet, but when the spirit is weak, it is easier for bad intentions aimed at you to find their target.

You must also stay "pure" by refraining from thinking negative thoughts about others, or allowing yourself to be influenced by the negative opinions of others. Mentally recite mantras to strengthen your spirit and to protect your mind.

This is a good time to discover the **power of mantras** or amulets camouflaged as auspicious products. The best are the **watches** we started designing several years ago, which contain moving mantras that simulate the continuous reciting of specific mantras. These are more powerful than we realize and this is positive programming of the best kind, creating an invisible protective aura without you even realizing!

DOG'S LOVE LUCK IN 2015

The Dog is definitely vulnerable to the *Peach Blossom* Star this year which makes you particularly romantic. You are likely even to view people and events in a very romantic way. Especially for those who are single and still unattached, the Dog is very likely to be actively seeking love.

The year 2015 is a decidedly ambivalent year for the Dog, but only because for many of you, it will be a question of doing the conventionally right thing or succumbing to sentiments that overcome you. There are instances where you could be tempted to throw caution to the winds and give in to the strong urge to allow some romance into your life.

Especially for those of you who are male and are holding responsible positions, this year can pose some challenges that you will find difficult to be decisive about. This is because when the star of peach blossom flies into your sector, it not only affects the vulnerabilities of the Dog it is especially potent when you are also male and are the patriarchal figure within your family.

For the Dog who is already married, the *Star of Peach Blossom* can also have a positive impact on your marriage OR it could cause you to be vulnerable to the *Flower of External Romance*. Other factors will come into play in your situation.

DOG'S WORK LUCK IN 2015

The Dog has a mixed bag when it comes to work luck. On the one hand, your success luck is weak, but on the other hand, your business luck benefits from the good fortune brought by the *Ho Tu* combination in your sector. Feng shui winds benefit you quite a bit this year and despite whatever may be troubling you mentally, this is not a bad year.

Indeed, the year 2015 augurs well for the Dog's work life – whether in a career, professional or business context. Success luck may be lacking, but there are other ways the year will bring you satisfaction and happiness. It is a good time to stay aware of meetings with people who may prove useful to you. There are new opportunities that can steer you in totally new directions that benefit you in the longer term. Allow your skill and goodwill with people to show you the way, because if there is one thing that benefits the Dog, it is the goodwill of long-forgotten allies and people whom you might have previously helped.

DOG'S BUSINESS LUCK IN 2015

The business outlook for the Dog hinges very much on the appearance of the Ho Tu combination of 4/9, which brings good business luck. Thus although this may not be an outstandingly successful year in terms of your success luck showing in your Elements Horoscope, nevertheless, excellent feng shui winds bring you opportunity for business success from another direction.

There is hence a good possibility for the *Ho Tu* to manifest something unexpected and very welcome, and you would benefit then to stay the course you are on. This is not something you need to spend time agonizing over. Just expect something quite spontaneous to develop for you that opens new directions of focus for you. This is most likely to happen for the **45 year old Metal Dog**. Remember that good fortune rarely if ever comes with a big bang; often, good fortune can take place without one even being aware that something great is happening.

CHAPTER 2
LUCK OF THE SHEEP YEAR 2015

*for those born
in the Year of the Dog*

LUCK OF THE
WOOD SHEEP YEAR 2015
A WELL-BALANCED YEAR

The Dog in 2015 is in a very relaxed mood. To some, you will seem ambivalent about many things but to others who know you well and are close to you, this simply reflects your need for a well-earned rest after some high energy years. Many of the Dog sign have been juggling various demands on your time; you have been working too hard and also travelling too much. But the Dog enjoys being relevant and useful to others. Being accommodating towards those counted as your friends is second nature to you.

Hence in spite of your wanting to take things a little easier, the Dog's continuing popularity will have you going through a sociable year. There will be many collective occasions, parties and get-together events that will continue to make demands on you. Life is thus going to be quite a whirl. But the Dog likes the social life.

The Dog sign is known for loyalty and spontaneous kindness towards others. This is not a sign that is madly ambitious for power or greedy for wealth, and in 2015, you are really more interested in romance and in expanding family ties. The younger ones amongst you could find yourselves involved in some sweet love affair, while the older ones will be organizing social occasions and partying till dawn.

The philosophy of the Dog for this year is clear; making love is more fun than making war, and partying beats working.

The Dog sign is also influenced by the *Star of the Peach Blossom*, which has landed in the sector that belongs to its sign. So this can easily become a year when you are literally showered with all kinds of loving, but mostly of the long-term kind that leads to matrimony or getting into a lived-in situation with someone.

Indeed, in terms of romantic entanglements - both of the frivolous kind as well as the serious sort - this Year of the Sheep should turn out to be quite an exceptional one for the Dog. It is a good year to marry or to exchange commitments with someone. It is a year that benefits the conscious coupling of lovers. Pull yourself together, lift yourself out of lethargy and get into the groove. It is that kind of year; you are sure to derive great pleasure from being in love, which gets your adrenalin flowing.

The Dog enjoys good business luck this year also - brought by the *Ho Tu* combination of 4/9 landing in your compass location. This is an outstanding aspect of your luck profile for the coming year.

Unfortunately however, the Dog's *lung ta* or personal Windhorse is showing a very bad reading this year. Success luck is not blowing your way. It seems that this is a year for taking things easy rather than pushing excessively hard for success to actualize.

Those of you wanting to work as hard as you play can nevertheless engage in rituals associated with raising the Windhorse. This might well be a good idea, especially as the year is offering a potentially auspicious scenario. There are exciting opportunities emerging and the Dog should try to make the most of the year's potential.

This year 2015, all five of the worldly elements of Water, Wood, Fire, Earth and Metal make their appearance in the Paht Chee chart. There are two yin and two yang pillars that reflect a stable and healthy balance of the primordial forces that influence the world's energy patterns.

We are likely to see an end to the severe weather extremes of previous years and interpersonal energies between people are expected to improve quite substantially. What is important is that all this reflects a new stability in the world's frequency vortexes. The year is nurturing, less conflict ridden and there are enough good fortune opportunities to benefit everyone sensitive to the new patterns of energies. It is a year when performing at one's best comes spontaneously; unlike last year when the energies of the world tended to be rough and tough, lacking the foundations needed for focused concentration.

2015 is different. It is a year when the big decisions taken by those in charge will be less aggressive and more conciliatory. Leaders will be less prone to autocratic or corrupt behaviour, and they will avoid causing discord or allowing conflicts to burst into dangerous confrontation. There will be fewer direct or open conflicts.

This makes the outlook far more encouraging than last year. There is room for compromise; reason for optimism.

Individual animal signs however are generally weaker than in previous years in terms of personal inner strength and confidence levels. Success in 2015 will depend on how positive one can be and also on how effectively one can motivate oneself, especially in work and business. Viewed from this perspective, the Dog must somehow depend on its latent passion for doing some good work to benefit others. This is the Achilles Heel of the Dog sign, as nothing will make the Dog get to working faster than when convinced he/she can benefit someone.

But the Dog will need to be focused and not succumb to a flightiness of attitude. Success does not come easy to you this year, so unless you are strongly motivated, you are unlikely to maintain any kind of momentum.

> The Dog can be too playful for its own good, although there are some powerful feng shui winds and indications that favour the more relaxed rather than the more intense approach to work.

It is preferable then for those whose lives are affected by yours to simply let you be and not cause you to become too intense or too driven this year.

Everyone should be reminded that unfortunately for 2015, the year is dominated by the extremely hostile, conflict-producing number 3 star in the center of the year's feng shui chart. This suggests that anger energy tends to explode at the slightest smallest provocation.

Be careful. It really is vital to keep rage energy under control. This is the most important affliction of the year, although the Dog is likely to be in full control.

> The Dog sign is not known to lose its temper easily or quickly. The Dog sign is also conciliatory in its attitude and approach towards disagreements. So you are unlikely to let anger energy have its way. You are good at walking away from conflict situations, although occasionally, those who wrong this sign can instigate you to become quite quarrelsome.

So do be mindful of the number 3 star. Take measures to keep it under wraps. Do this and the year will turn out favourable for you. Those depending on you to set the tone for the year will take their cue from you. For instance, if you are in an influential position such as being the head of an organization or simply playing the father or mother role in the family, it is imperative not to allow the conflict star of 3 derail you.

There are some very auspicious indications brought by the stars of the 24 Mountains. There is also the presence of the four *Ho Tu* combinations, and the **Dog location of Northwest** is one of the four locations playing host to one of the Ho Tu this year. This means that the Dog sign benefits directly from this year's Ho Tu phenomenon. Nevertheless, like everyone else, the Dog needs to restrain from succumbing to temper tantrums, and wherever possible, to take a deep breath before using your authority to bully others. Those of you in positions of power must subdue any urge to be unkind.

> **SUBDUE ANGER ENERGY:** Most importantly, whether you believe in feng shui or not, everyone in 2015 must subdue the number 3 star in the center of the feng shui chart – this, and the wearing of an **Anti-Anger Amulet**, are the keys to ensuring a smooth ride through 2015.

Once you are able to avoid being affected by this major obstacle of 2015, you will be in an excellent position to take fullest advantage of the year's well-balanced Paht Chee, which brings harmonious frequencies to the year.

In addition to all five elements being present, there are two pairs of astrological "secret friends" comprising the **Sheep** and the **Horse** in the Year and Hour Pillars respectively, and the **Tiger** (Month Pillar) and the **Boar** (Day Pillar) in the other two pillars.

The Harmony Friends of 2015 form different ally and friendship groupings within the year's defining Paht Chee Chart, making all relationships go more smoothly. The year's Paht Chee also alleviates angst brought by the Flying Star chart, which is dominated by the #3 quarrelsome star.

The presence of **astrological friendships** in the Paht Chee is a rare luck-bringing phenomenon that indicates peace and auspicious energies for the year. These four animal signs will enjoy the luck of **social popularity** this year. Their appearance in the year's Paht Chee is considered a good sign. Also take note that the Tiger and Horse are allies, while the Sheep and Boar are also allies. Thus all four animals in the year's Paht Chee are "related" in a cosmically harmonious manner.

Connectivity between people will tend to soften; resentments and hostility are effectively diffused. Good sense will prevail despite quick temper tantrums and violent eruptions of anger energy, although this too tends to dissipate as the year progresses.

Display the crest of the **Harmony Friends of 2015** in your living room area to engender harmony within the family and at the workplace to create harmonious interface at work.

Note that:
- The Horse & Sheep bring **great sexual passion**
- The Boar & Tiger bring **hidden wealth**
- The Horse & Tiger allies **bring hidden power**
- The Boar & Sheep bring **skillful diplomacy**

The placement of these four animals ensures that in spite of unreasonable behaviour causing antipathy to rise to the fore brought by the hostile #3, this can be controlled by the harmonizing forces of the year's Paht Chee.

This year's Eight Characters chart ensures that the social, business & friendship environment of the year stays harmonious and peaceful. Those with goodwill intentions are stronger than those who are hot-headed. The doves will outnumber the hawks!

This is a good indication as it means the trend towards increasing violence and hostility has been stopped and is thus cooling. Also this year's patriarchal energy which reflects the attitudes of the men in leadership positions tends to be loving and placating as it comes under the influence of the loving energies of the *Peach Blossom*. Men in leadership positions and within families tend to be conciliatory and kinder.

LUCK OF THE EARTH SIGNS

This year, the four "Earth" signs – **Ox, Dragon, Sheep** and **Dog** – enjoy good life force but weak spirit essence. All four signs register a range of different strengths in their personal *lung ta* or Windhorse, and of the four, the Ox is the sign that enjoys the strongest success luck, followed by the Dragon and the Sheep. Unfortunately, of the four, it is the sign of the Dog that shows the most disturbingly negative indications. Your *lung ta* is at a very bad level and your spirit essence - which is a measure of your confidence - is also at a negative level.

Actually all four Earth signs have weak spirit essence and suffer from self doubt and a lack of confidence in 2015. But Earth represents resources this year; and in such a well-balanced year, **this becomes an important success factor.**

THE LUCK OF THE ALLY GROUPINGS

When we examine the success luck of the **Dog and its allies**, the **Tiger** and **Horse**, we find that they too are affected by weak personal Windhorses. Thus this grouping is likely to find it quite tough to bring work projects to a satisfactory completion. Promotion prospects also look dismal, although of the three, it is the Tiger who is most likely to achieve upward mobility professionally. This is because of the three, it is the Tiger whose courage and confidence is the strongest. Nevertheless, success is elusive. This does not mean there is no success – only that climbing uphill requires effort.

TRINITY OF INDEPENDENTS

Meanwhile, the grouping made up of the **Dragon, Rat** and **Monkey** also needs to adjust to some new realities in 2015. Having been on a roll for these past couple of years, the coming year will see these signs running out of steam. The *Competitors* of the Zodiac show indications that energy levels are weakening, and for the Dragon and Rat, this affects their ability to generate inner confidence. The Monkey however is full of energy, enjoying superb life force and inner essence. So the Dragon and Rat would do well to tap the luck of their ally the Monkey.

TRINITY OF COMPETITORS

The **Rabbit, Sheep** and **Boar** belong to the trinity of signs known as the **Diplomats**. Of the three, the **Boar** and **Sheep** are going through a tougher time than the **Rabbit**. So the Boar and Sheep are advised to lean on the Rabbit. This year, all three signs have weak *lung-ta*, in other words, their success luck is very low. For them, we advise inviting the **Windhorse** into their space to strengthen their success luck, or better yet, participate in the Windhorse-Raising ritual. This comprises of releasing into the skies helium-filled balloons that have been stamped with the image of the Windhorse flag!

TRINITY
OF
DIPLOMATS

Meanwhile, the **Tiger** and its allies, the **Dog** and **Horse** are also affected by their weak personal Windhorse. This grouping finds it tough to bring work projects to satisfactory completion. Promotion prospects look dismal, although of the three, it is the Tiger who is most likely to achieve upward mobility professionally. This is because of the three, it is the Tiger whose courage and confidence is the strongest. Nevertheless, success for all three can be elusive. This does not mean there is no success – only that success cannot be instant. This is a year best spent building than completing.

The **Ox, Rooster** and **Snake** are the only trinity of signs that seem to enjoy powerful assertive Windhorse energies that take them to new heights this year. These three signs are the scholars and visionaries, all three of whom are capable of seeing beyond the obvious. Of the three, it will be the Ox who is weakest and the Rooster who is the most afflicted; and it is the Snake who will rise the highest.

TRINITY OF INTELLECTUALS

THE ELEMENT OF WEALTH LUCK IN 2015 IS <u>WOOD</u>

For all signs, when it comes to wealth luck in 2015, the element to activate and strengthen is Wood. Note there is plenty of wealth luck indicated for the year, both direct as well as indirect wealth. There is also a good store of *hidden wealth* emerging. It is very beneficial and thus advisable to place the symbolic **Forest of Wealth Globe** at the front of the house, as this signifies the presence of the Wood element energy. This wonderful enhancer features a glorious cluster of trees together with three sheep by the mountain unlocking gold. It brings wonderful financial stability to the household.

It is especially helpful for the **57 year old Earth Dog** who will need the extra Wood element energy to strengthen its wealth luck. For the **69 year old Fire Dog**, this year brings bonanza wealth luck and Wood will fuel the Fire further.

THE ELEMENT OF POWER LUCK IN 2015 IS FIRE

In 2015, the significance of Fire energy is that it brings power and recognition luck. These are important attributes of the success factor. There is *direct* as well as *indirect* power luck this year, because there is both obvious and hidden Fire in the chart. It is excellent then to install strong Fire energy in the home and especially in the center of the home, because the Fire element also effectively subdues the hostile and harmful number 3 star in the center.

HARNESSING THE FIVE POWERS:
In 2015, everyone will need greater authority to get things done; simply because the 3 in the centre generates aggravating hassles and obstacles that block the success of projects and activities. If you are in a managerial position then you will really benefit by carrying a set of the **Five Element Ru Yi Wands** which we have

filled with secret dharani mantras and studded with gems to help you develop the five powers:

+ The **Fire Ruyi Wand (red)** enhances your *power of speech*, the ability to persuade others and have them come under your influence.
+ The **Earth Ruyi Wand (yellow)** enhances your *power of knowledge*. This ensures that you always have the right information to make good decisions and are not easily fooled.
+ The **Water Ruyi Wand (blue)** enhances your *power to control money*, helping to ensure you are in full control of where your finances go.
+ The **Wood Ruyi Wand (green)** enhances your *power to expand*, giving you the courage and resources to develop all areas of your life.
+ The **Metal Ruyi Wand (white)** brings the *power of mentors*, attracting influential benefactors that give you unwavering support.

INVITING KING GESAR FOR SUCCESS

The Dog's success luck is badly affected by the very bad reading on the personal *lung ta* this year. This indicates that whatever success you want this year is going to be tough. When your *lung ta* is so weak, it has to be made strong and then activated. The Dog is definitely going to find that all the trimmings of success - the recognition and the respect luck - is sure to be seriously weakened as well.

> When there is a lack of success luck, you will find that previously warm friends who could not get enough of you become lukewarm. What hurts also is the weakness of the Dog's spirit essence as well.

You will need then focus strongly on giving your inner spirit a boost. Try to create a mindset of success. This mentally attracts happiness events to manifest for you. A positive mindset is the best kind of feng shui because it establishes the mental energy that will help you persevere, despite it being harder to achieve what you want. In the case of the Dog, staying positive this year requires additional effort because your spirit essence is weak. Work then at motivating yourself strongly and then take note of what you need to do to strengthen your *lung ta* to enhance your success potential this year.

MANIFESTING SUCCESS LUCK

Strengthening your *lung ta* means strengthening your personal Windhorse, and the best way to do this is to invite the legendary King Gesar of Ling, the powerful

warrior manifestation of the Enlightened Masters into your home. The presence of any image of King Gesar helps create the energy for **serious success luck** to materialize in the most beneficial way for you. This is because King Gesar's Horse is the Windhorse itself. With King Gesar supporting you, your work life will be smoother. Success comes more easily; there may be the odd aggravation but these are minor setbacks. With a strong Windhorse, you will be resilient to setbacks and you will benefit from a renewed determination to stay on top of whatever you need to do or get done.

Mostly, you will find that you can actualize what you set out to achieve, to mine the great mountain of blessings that stays open all through the Year of the Sheep. This is a great year to invite King Gesar into your home because with his help, you can be more mindful of growth opportunities that abound this year. The Year of the Sheep opens a mountain of wish-granting jewels to the world.

King Gesar is a commanding and legendary figure of the Himalayas and the people of the countries that span this fabulous mountain range. From Tibet to China and all the countries in between, there is great devotion for this great Protector.

King Gesar is considered a powerful warrior
monarch who brings continuing success
to the residents of any home with his
image. He rides his powerful steed, and
in his hands he carries weapons to defeat
demon spirits that bring illness, setbacks
and obstacles that block personal success
luck. King Gesar's presence is strongly
awakened when you recite his **mantra**
and his **four-line invocation**.

KYE / DODDUN KUNDRUB DRALHA THUWO CHE
RIGSUM PADMEI GYUTHRUL SENGCHEN GYAL
NORBU DRADUL KADOD PHONYER CHE
SOLLO CHODDO SAMDON LHUNDRUB DZOD

Kye! Wishfulfilling Protector of Great Power
Great Lion, Emanation of Padmasambava and
Three Great Bodhisattvas,
Manjushri, Avalokiteshvara, and Vajrapani
With your Dharma Protectors and Tamer of Maras
Please accept our offerings and fulfill all our wishes.

Here we combine astrological readings with cosmic feng shui rituals to ensure that the year will be special and motivational!

SECOND HALF OF THE YEAR IMPROVES

The Sheep Year 2015 is extremely well-balanced, but the first half of the year is influenced by destructive Month and Year Pillars. This is a time of the year when the Wood element destroys the Earth element. The first half of the year is therefore more difficult in terms of getting projects off the ground. There are setbacks, and resources get used up more quickly than they can be replenished.

In the second half of the year however, we see the heavenly stem elements of the DAY and HOUR pillars producing the earthly branch elements. That is when the tempo increases and many will find new opportunities opening up, with things moving a lot more smoothly.

In this Year of the Sheep, the element of WOOD dominates the Paht Chee chart, indicating the preponderance of good growth energy.

Wood is what brings progress, a branching outwards of good energy. This strengthens the element of Fire, which ripens into great good fortune for the end of the year. Wood needs Water to generate continuous growth, and there is not a great deal of Water in the main chart of 2015, but the good news is that there is also no shortage of Water, since the monthly luck pillars bring sufficient water to fuel the energy of growth.

> The chart shows that there is WATER through the Spring months, even though the lunar new year coming so late causes there to be no *lap chun*.

To balance out the missing *lap chun*, it is beneficial to welcome in all the symbols of spring into the home during the fifteen days of the Lunar New Year. Carry the Spring Amulet of 2015 which has been embellished with all the important spring symbols sourced from the Lineage texts. Having this amulet near you throughout spring will jump-start growth energy for you.

It is also beneficial to **keep wearing red** and to surround yourself with red, as the energy of Fire is what expands the confidence factor within households. Many individual signs this year suffer from a lack of life force and inner spirit energies, so it is beneficial to enhance these important dimensions of individual luck in 2015.

Happily for the Dog, you do not lack the important life force energy so from this perspective, your personal luck strength is not weak. But **Fire benefits you** as it is what enhances your intrinsic element of Earth.

TO STRENGTHEN YOUR LIFE FORCE

Wearing gold makes your Life Force stronger this year; it simulates the Mother Earth producing nurturing energy for the son. Wearing gold is what will strengthen everyone's life force in 2015. **This is the key tip for the year.** For those who cannot or do not like wearing gold, you can wear silver or other metals, but gold (yellow or white) is generally regarded as the premier symbol of the Metal element.

You should generate as much powerful life force chi energy as you can, as this gives you the ability to activate smooth-flowing abundance. When your Life Force is strong, you can overcome any number of hurdles. Many of Asia's communities including the Chinese and Indians love wearing gold because this is a metal that can overcome a great many luck afflictions.

Wearing gold is so beneficial that it has become a traditional symbol for generating good fortune luck. Indeed, the Chinese always wear gold when they wish to activate prosperity luck, especially when a child is born.

TO STRENGTHEN YOUR INNER SPIRIT

Your inner spirit is low this year and needs to bestrengthened. To add strength to your Inner Spirit in 2015, it is beneficial to wear **some kind of gemstone** as this symbolizes the Earth element. This is because in 2015, the element of year's Spirit Essence is Fire, which produces Earth in the cycle. Hence wearing a gemstone to signify Earth is extremely beneficial.

The Dog must strengthen its spirit essence; doing so will enhance your ability to cope with whatever spiritual poison arrows that may get sent your way.

We are currently living through a degenerate period when the bad intentions of people tend to crystallize. The temptation to indulge in spiritual warfare is strong, and many succumb to it. As a result, we see the rise of dark forces, and it is truly vital to strengthen your inner spirit essence so that you are shielded by strong and invisible protective energies.

When you recite mantras regularly, this protects your mind and keeps you safe, as the mantras imbue you with the clear thought that you are under the protective refuge of the enlightened beings. In 2015 however, if you can also wear **some kind of crystalline gemstone** – diamonds, sapphires, rubies, emeralds or tourmalines – this would be extremely beneficial. When you wear gemstones and you recite mantras, the energy of the mantras will stay embedded inside these gemstones, hence the more you recite and wear, the more protected you will be.

KING GESAR MANTRA RING

This mantra ring has been specially designed to enhance one's inner essence and life force. In 2015, the majority of animal signs do not enjoy superlative spiritual strength, so wearing a mantra ring would be most beneficial.

PAHT CHEE CHART 2015
YEAR OF THE WOOD SHEEP

HOUR	DAY	MONTH	YEAR
YANG WOOD WOOD brings WEALTH	**YIN METAL** METAL brings ALLIES	**YANG EARTH** DESTRUCTIVE	**YIN WOOD** WOOD brings WEALTH
PRODUCTIVE hidden YIN EARTH FIRE brings POWER	**PRODUCTIVE** hidden YANG WOOD WATER brings INTELLIGENCE	hidden YANG EARTH hidden YANG FIRE WOOD brings WEALTH	**DESTRUCTIVE** hidden YIN WOOD EARTH brings RESOURCES hidden YIN FIRE
YANG **FIRE** **HORSE**	**YIN** **WATER** **BOAR**	**YANG** **WOOD** **TIGER**	**YIN** **EARTH** **SHEEP**
STAR OF POWERFUL MENTORS			

The Paht Chee chart of 2015 is happily a very well-balanced chart with all five elements present and with the predominant element being **Wood**. The key element of the year is **strong Yin Metal**. Here is a summary of the year's Paht Chee chart and the potential influences it exerts on the year's fortunes.

WOOD ELEMENT
There are 2 Yang Wood and 1 Yin Wood in the main chart, making a total of 3 Wood elements. This indicates strong growth chi energy for the world. The Wood element represents the year's wealth potential,

so this is truly a promising indication. There is definitely a good deal of wealth luck in 2015 and this of course reflects the Sheep opening the treasures of the mountains to the world. This is very auspicious. In addition, there is one hidden Yin Wood and one hidden Yang Wood, suggesting there is also hidden wealth available. This strengthens the prosperity potential of the year. Displaying the **Forest of Wealth Globe** captures this perfectly.

EARTH ELEMENT

There is **one Yang Earth** and **one Yin Earth** in the chart, and **a hidden Yang Earth** and **a hidden Yin Earth**. In all, there is the presence of four Earth elements and this points to 2015 benefitting from there being sufficient resources to fuel the growth of the world's productive activities. There is hidden as well as obvious availability of resources. This too is an auspicious indication as Earth produces Metal, which is the vitality element of the year.

There is no shortage of physical resources and there is also the will to increase productivity this year. Focus shifts from the aggressive energies of previous years into more productive activities this year. This is the characteristic of Sheep Years and with such a good supporting Paht Chee chart, the year should see the ripening of pleasant surprises for many people. The year then is a good year and it is up to individual signs to take fullest advantage of the year.

METAL, FIRE & WATER ELEMENTS

There is one of each of these elements in the main chart, hence creating a balanced chart with nothing missing for the year.

The element of Fire indicates *power, authority and recognition.* In 2015, Fire energy brings luminosity to the year's good fortunes, as it basically strengthens the inner spirit of the year. With the presence of Fire, there is determination and good support from those in leadership positions to encourage the productive direction of the year. The good news is that in addition to the single Fire in the main chart, there are also **two hidden Fire**, one of which is yin, and one yang. These are lucky indications.

The single Metal element signifies *friendly, competitive pressures.* There is cooperation rather than competition this year, so here we will witness a pulling back of the aggressive energies of the immediately preceding year. The Sheep is a docile creature, more skillful than the Horse in staying calm, so this brings a year when conciliatory gestures will prevail over the hostility and aggression of the Horse Year. As there is only one Metal, it is again beneficial to wear gold to enhance and strengthen the presence of this element.

ENHANCING INTELLIGENCE: The single Water element signifies *intelligence and creativity*. There is not much of this vital attribute in 2015, but at least it is not missing. But this does suggest that it is beneficial for those needing the attributes of water in 2015 i.e. intelligence and educational prowess to either **carry a symbolic droplet of water** (as a keychain) or place the **Lotus Root with water enhancer** by their desk as they study, do their homework, write their research paper or do any kind of writing work.

This tip is especially beneficial for those who are in an examination year or applying for a place in College or preparing for an important scholarship or entrance interview.

DESTRUCTIVE PILLARS

The Paht Chee of 2015 comprises Year and Month Pillars that are made up of **Wood and Earth.** These two elements have a destructive relationship and they bring less lucky indications to the first half of the year. The destructive pillars are Yin and Yang pillars.

The Yin Year Pillar has the stem of Wood destroying the Branch of Earth. This indicates some naturally-occurring severe storms dislodging Earth at the start of the year. **The Yang Month Pillar** has the branch Wood destroying the stem Earth. This suggests an unfortunate time when accidents caused by human errors can occur. Note that in these two destructive pillars, it is the Wood element that is dominating, and Wood signifies wealth in 2015.

MONTH	YEAR
YANG EARTH DESTRUCTIVE	**YIN WOOD** WOOD brings WEALTH
hidden YANG EARTH hidden YANG FIRE WOOD brings WEALTH **YANG WOOD TIGER**	**DESTRUCTIVE** hidden YIN WOOD EARTH brings RESOURCES hidden YIN FIRE **YIN EARTH SHEEP**

Thus while the pillars are destructive, the dominance of Wood indicates that there is wealth to be found in the ground. Wood destroying Earth always suggests the discovery of some kind of treasures of the earth, and although this comes at a cost, nevertheless, it is also indicative of **new wealth emerging**.

PRODUCTIVE PILLARS

In the Day and Hour Pillars, we see Yin and Yang pillars having a productive relationship. These are the auspicious pillars of the year. Thus the **Yin Day Pillar** shows Metal producing Water. This suggests that the third quarter will be a time when there is a flowering of creativity, new technologies being launched and perhaps also some major breakthrough being made in the sciences that benefit people.

HOUR	DAY
YANG WOOD WOOD brings WEALTH	**YIN METAL** METAL brings ALLIES
PRODUCTIVE hidden YIN EARTH FIRE brings POWER	PRODUCTIVE hidden YANG WOOD WATER brings INTELLIGENCE
YANG FIRE HORSE	**YIN WATER BOAR**

This will define the year as one with the Day Pillar playing a pivotal role. Finally, in the **Yang Hour Pillar**, we see the heavenly stem of Wood producing the Earthly branch of Fire, and this brings the manifestation of stability in many countries.

Fire is the element of power, and when it occurs as a culmination of the year and within a productive relationship of the year's dominant element of Wood, it is an auspicious indication. We should witness a good number of benevolent developments by year end in 2015.

Note that there are no missing elements in the 2015 chart, and both Yin and Yang pillars are present. These are indications of stability; there is a fundamental feeling of wellness through the year.

HIDDEN POWERFUL MENTOR STAR

This year, there is one **astrological star** brought by the Paht Chee chart, but it is hidden and available only to those who energize for its presence to manifest. This is the **Powerful Mentor Star,** which brings significant hidden assistance to those lucky enough to manifest it. This is an auspicious star, but it is not easily detected as it is a hidden star. The star is created by the hidden elements of the earthly branch of Sheep which combines with the Tiger Earthly branch of the chart. In Chinese astrological analysis, much is made of the presence of "mentor" luck. This is the power of the *gui ren,* the influential friend who opens doorways to greatness and prosperity.

> The Chinese believe that often, the main success factor in the career of any young scholar is the presence of the *gui ren,* the helpful mentor. There are special rituals offered by Taoist temples that help young men and women actualize a mentor *gui ren* in their careers.

These are popular rituals, which are practised to this day. We might be very modern in our outlook, but many still appreciate having *gui ren* luck, as it is really very beneficial. It brings a powerful godfather figure, a secret benefactor, a helpful friend - someone who lends an unseen but beneficial helping influence that lifts you high on your career path.

To have this star in the year's Paht Chee suggests that anyone can activate for the presence of the *gui ren* in their lives. If you can manifest such a mentor type person to help you in your career path, it will allow you to make progress by leaps and bounds. The *gui ren* can also aid those of you who are in business.

This kind of luck brings influential people taking a liking to you, noticing you and lending you a helping hand. You will always have someone to speak up for you, and in times of crisis, there will be someone to pull you out of difficulties.

In feng shui terms, this means that in 2015, it is beneficial to have the presence of an **older figure sitting on a Tiger** and **surrounded by the presence of Yin Fire element** on your desk. This is what will bring the heavenly mentor into your life. It is for this reason that the traditional Wealth God of the Chinese is almost always shown sitting on a Tiger. The *gui ren* symbolic presence is not an easy figure to get, as it is not readily available, and indeed in the old days, such symbolic enhancers were specially commissioned.

For the Dog Lady, you can harness Gui Ren luck of the year simply by carrying the **Mirror to Attract Benefactors**. This magical mirror is imbued with images of Precious Queen, Precious Minister and Precious General to attract the luck of powerful mentors who will support you in your career and business. Use them when attending dinner functions where important people will be in attendance.

THE FLYING STAR CHART OF 2015

Chinese astrology and feng shui sciences are rich with **nuanced systems of divination,** which we can use to investigate how our luck will turn out as we mature over the passage of time. It is natural to want to ensure continuing good fortune for ourselves and our families, and as the energies of the world change with each new year, it really is beneficial to investigate how the new patterns of energies will affect our lives and our luck.

Where possible, we should do our best to strengthen all the positive energies and weaken all the afflictive energies. What is involved in the practice of feng shui here is to apply the art of placement, i.e. with good fortune symbols put correctly so they activate good fortune, and also using powerful remedial symbols to suppress bad luck energy.

The correct placement of new symbols brought into the home during the New Year will ensure your path through the twelve months of 2015 is smooth and harmonious.

Most important for the Dog is to strengthen your spirit essence, which is low in 2015, as this complements the presence of symbolic enhancing energy within your home environment; then your annual success and prosperity luck will operate at similar frequencies, ensuring a smooth flow of auspicious luck through the year. The ancients cracked the code of the Universe when they succeeded in tracking the transformation of cosmic energies, deciphering the annual and period changes in energy patterns and recording them into precious lineage texts for use by succeeding generations.

Today, we use the charts and methods recorded many centuries ago as part of our feng shui practice to ensure serenity in our lives, successfully avoiding trouble, accidents, poor judgement and mishaps, and the kind of misfortune that can destroy our peace of mind.

When we know how the energies of the Universe change in its effect on the different animal signs and the different houses from year to year, it helps us avoid becoming a victim of injustice, falling ill from disease, experiencing failure at work, or facing all kinds of adversities that are not only unpleasant, but that also cause great suffering.

Usually, misfortune and failure is caused by bad luck, which in turn is caused by the cosmic forces that swirl around the environment leading to upheavals in the universal balance. These act through the four elements of the cosmic Universe i.e. Earth, Fire, Water and Air, which manifest through Wood, Rocks, the Sun and the Moon. These are manipulated by the connectivity of the five elements – Fire, Earth, Metal, Water and Wood – which arrange themselves into patterns of energy, where those who know how, can decipher and work through to find solutions that alleviate bad luck.

There is simple bad luck and there is severe misfortune; knowing how to avoid suffering or at least how to reduce the impact of misfortune is really worth taking trouble over.

Knowing how to investigate the feng shui chart, which reveals the luck attributes of each of the corners of manmade houses and buildings according to the way the feng shui winds blow during each new year, is thus a valuable skill indeed.

The Flying Star chart reveals the pattern of energy changes that take place each year so effectively that for those who know how to make use of the knowledge, it can seem to work like magic. The accuracy of the moving numbers in revealing the placement of new energy forces is truly amazing, as year after year, we repeatedly discover just how useful knowing the secrets of the Flying Star chart can be in helping us navigate through illnesses, misfortune, setbacks and obstacles. More importantly, we find that the Flying Star chart also helps us to strongly magnify specific kinds of good fortune luck simply by correctly energizing specific corners and sectors of the home.

We also discover that while it is important to render good feng shui to the different spaces of our homes, hence practicing the space dimension of feng shui, it is the mindfulness we place on the **time dimension of feng shui** that is so pivotal in helping us negotiate through the pitfalls of life's journey, thereby avoiding the big misfortunes.

THE POWER OF CURES

It is the power of the remedies and cures that has proven to be the most magical of all. These are the **countering symbols** – each designed according to recommendations described and explained in the lineage texts, and each placed in specific spaces defined by their compass locations within any abode.

In the past eighteen years since we have gone deeper into investigating the esoteric sciences that complement feng shui practice, we have discovered the all-important *spiritual dimensions of feng shui* as well.

Thus we have relied increasingly on the sacred images, syllables, symbols, tools and colours to lend even greater strength to overcoming distressing conditions brought by negative astrological winds. Misfortune can cause great suffering, and it is with the motivation to help override these kinds of sufferings that we write these books each year. Happily, our books have encouraged others to give voices to the efficacy of the Flying Star chart.

We were the first to strongly emphasize the importance of studying the feng shui implications of this important chart. But today, the feng shui chart of each New Year is given prominence by many other feng shui experts around the world.

The chart changes each year, and serious study of the chart is required before cures or enhancers can be designed and used effectively. There is also the element of connectivity with other astrological charts that reveal other influences on the destiny outcomes of the year.

We go further to investigate the interaction between the Flying Stars and the 24 Mountains stars of the year, as this too changes from year to year, and this is addressed in detail in the next section. This makes our destiny readings of each new year better nuanced and more complete, because of course, no animal sign has all good or all bad luck.

> There are degrees of good fortune and misfortune; the charts and numbers, star influences and elements combine differently for different people.

It is important not to make the mistake of thinking there are only 12 kinds of fortune for all the people of the world. Indeed, just in the animal signs alone, there are 60 possibilities as we input in the 5 elements to the animal signs. We also input the five types of **Element Luck** of each sign and we consider the impact of the Paht Chee elements, the 24 Mountains stars, as well as the the *Ho Tu* combinations.

There is also the influence exerted by the homes and apartments that people live in! We bring the relevant findings of the different indicators and summarize our analysis in a user-friendly way. You decide how deep you want to go to investigate your fortune and feng shui for the coming year, although what has been included here is already more than sufficient to ensure for you a secure and successful ride through 2015.

We go to great lengths to help readers get the placement of symbolic cures and lucky symbols done correctly. This affects the time effects on the feng shui of your homes and offices. It is not difficult to get good feng shui when you place remedies and activators correctly. Once you understand the fundamental basis of the recommendations, you can do this easily.

BE CAREFUL OF FAKES: We take great care in designing the cures correctly, so readers really must be careful of fakes, which ignore the secret vital details that go into the design and material composition of our feng shui cures. Especially in the making of our amulets and talismans that contain special syllables and sacred mantras, it is important to ensure we get the syllables and symbols absolutely right.

MONTHLY READINGS

We place a great deal of emphasis on **monthly luck**, and especially in identifying the troublesome months for you, so that you stay alert during the more trying time periods. There is a whole section in the book focused exclusively on the monthly readings of luck in the categories of health, wealth, career, relationships and personal development. Letters written to us from our many readers tell us this section of the book is useful for negotiating through the difficult months of the year, when you may encounter illness, vicious corporate politics, annoying jealousies or other kinds of misfortune. We always give a solution for problems encountered!

Everyone can stay fully updated with the good and bad energy of each month. The feng shui winds of each new year are always different, in quality and in strength. Astrological indications for the twelve signs also change. Your luck patterns can bring drastic negative consequences and it is always good to be prepared so you know how to mitigate the consequences of bad winds.

No one is immune because there are so many categories of luck, and their patterns of changes are cyclical, with many interacting and interlocking in different ways. These books summarize the salient points of your luck profile, and they are all you need to stay connected to the time dimension of feng shui that affects your particular sign.

FLYING STAR CHART 2015
YEAR OF THE WOOD SHEEP

SE
SOUTH
SW
ILLNESS ENERGY
2
ENERGY OF BETRAYAL
7
FUTURE PROSPERITY
9
TAI SUI
EAST
VICTORY STAR
1
good judgement luck
HOSTILITY
ANGER ENERGY
3
strong power luck
THREE KILLINGS
5
WEST
HEAVEN LUCK
6
AUSPICIOUS WINDS
8
PEACH BLOSSOM
4
good business luck
NE
NORTH
NW

Here is the feng shui chart for 2015 – it shows you the energy patterns that influence the destiny and feng shui of the coming Year of the Wood Sheep. At first glance, the chart can be quite intimidating, but as you take note of the numbers inside each of the nine little squares that make up the chart, and you know that these numbers bring different things and have different strengths in each new year, you will begin to appreciate and understand the energy of the different sectors of your home or office, categorized according to the eight directions of the compass.

The idea is to mentally superimpose this chart onto your home, or into each room, using the actual compass directions of your home/room to anchor the corners. Stand in the center of your home and take directions. You need to identify the center of your home and also each sector of your home.

When you match the actual corners of your home to the chart according to the compass directions, you will see how your doors, especially your main door, and how each of the bedrooms are affected by the energies of the year indicated by the number(s) that fly into each compass sector. (You may find it easier to work with a pre-drawn layout of your home with the compass sectors clearly marked out.)

The chart has a center grid as well as eight surrounding grids. There is thus a center sector and 8 sectors that surround it, each corresponding to the four cardinal and four secondary directions. Every sector is influenced by a number from 1 to 9. These numbers mean different kinds of luck trends and tendencies. Our interpretations rely on the meanings of the numbers, on the strength of the numbers, on how the elements of the numbers interact with the elements of the sectors, and on how the Period 8 numbers interact with the annual numbers. We also consider the astrological impact of heavenly stems and the 12 animal signs.

To benefit fully from the analysis, it is best if you already know the different sectors of your home. You must know the compass directions of the different corners. Use a **good compass** to take directions from the center of the home, then mark out the different compass sectors of your living and work spaces.

The advice given here is meant to make it easy for you create lovely, fresh new feng shui in your home to harmonize with the energies of 2015.

We are using the art of placement to ensure that the correct symbolic cures and enhancers are used to generate vortexes of energy that subdue the afflictions in particular sectors OR magnify good fortune in other sectors.

You will feel much better after the placement changes as you throw out last year's cures (which have absorbed so much negative energy, it is best to throw them into a large river or lake) and bring in new remedies that have the vitality and vigour of new cures. You will feel more confident when you know you are being safeguarded with new cures that work so well against the major afflictive energies of the New Year.

The advice given for each compass sector applies to every level of the home. Note also that Stupas and all other sacred objects should not be thrown away, but instead, placed on your altars or in a high place.

And finally, remember that feng shui is the **Art of Placement!**

THE NUMBERS 1 TO 9

Every one of the numbers corresponds to an I Ching trigram, symbolizes an aspiration, signifies one of the five elements and has a feng shui meaning. The numbers also vary in strength according to where they fly to each year. Please do not mix up this annual chart and its placement of numbers in each sector with that of the Flying Star chart that has been worked out for your house. This Annual Flying Star chart is not the same as your House Flying Star chart with its water stars and mountain stars. So please do not get confused by the different charts.

Updating the feng shui of your house is practising TIME FENG SHUI and this will ensure that your good fortune continues and that nothing interferes with it during each new year.

You may have feng shui-ed your home exceptionally well and even spent a small fortune on the best Feng Shui Masters, but if you do not update your feng shui according to the new year's Flying Star and other charts, you *can* get hit by afflictive energies, especially if your main door, bedroom or office is directly hit by an afflictive star number in that year. Feng shui is a dynamic practice. The time dimension must not be ignored!

First step is to *identify* where all the afflictive and auspicious numbers of the year have flown to within your home.

Second step is to know what *remedies* you need to place in each of the afflicted corners to suppress the negative impact of the numbers.

Third step is to *awaken* the energy of sectors that have auspicious numbers.

Placement of cures and enhancers are done for each of the nine sectors, but the effect is felt by the entire household and throughout the whole house!

For annual updates, you must suppress afflictive star numbers and energize lucky auspicious stars. Prominence is placed on the annual number itself. For the different months of the year, we examine the month numbers to see how they interact with the annual numbers.

The placement of monthly cures can be moved around from month to month. For instance, a cure against the monthly illness star can move from sector to sector to track the illness star. But the annual cure for the illness star must stay where it is placed at start of the year.

The annual flying stars stay in the same locations throughout the year but monthly stars move to different sectors each month. Thus it is so vital to track the movement of the stars and place your cures in the correct sectors accordingly.

THE FLYING STAR FENG SHUI CHART OF 2015 IS RULED BY THE NUMBER 3

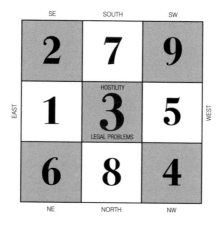

This is the quarrelsome Wood star, which brings **severe conflicts, misunderstandings and legal problems**. The effect of the number 3 star is usually severe, causing a great deal of aggravation and suffering. It was very strong in the previous two years, as it is a **Wood star** and it was in the East and Southeast, which are **Wood sectors**. In the center, which is an Earth sector, it is even stronger, as Wood destroys Earth. Also, the Year and Month Pillars of this year's Paht Chee chart has Wood destroying Earth – hence strengthening the destructive and quarrelsome energy of Wood.

This coincidental matching with the year's Paht Chee chart suggests that it is **really vital** to suppress the number 3 star in the center of your house.

Not doing so is sure to unleash the hostile energy of the number 3 star. The whole family can literally be at war! You will fight over the silliest, smallest things. Spouses will go to war with each other, as will siblings and other family members. The effect of the number 3 star is enormously unpleasant, and even though you may be aware of this, the energy is so quarrelsome you simply cannot help yourself. Sometimes, the number 3 star can have very tragic consequences as families get broken up and long-lasting conflicts get created.

LEGAL ENTANGLEMENTS

The number 3 star also causes households to be at war with their neighbours and business associates. You might find yourself entangled in legal problems or embroiled in a court case – usually over matters that can be quite easily solved in other ways, but because of the number 3 affliction, both sides get stubborn, dig their heels in and fight. It is really a very unpleasant affliction and we strongly urge you to suppress it at all costs. Make sure there are no moving objects or even the presence of tinkling windchimes in the center sector, as these are symbols that will strengthen the hostility vibes. Keeping the center of the home well lit with **bright lights** will help, as does the presence of **red carpets** and **red cushion covers**. The colour red signifies the Fire element, which exhausts the Wood element of the number 3 star.

> **For those born in years of the Dog,** your intrinsic element is Earth, which is weaker than Wood. In fact, Wood has the potential to destroy Earth. The number 3 star can be dangerous to the Dog. This means that you can be at the mercy of the number 3 star, because Wood destroys Earth. So those born in Dog years need to subdue the anger energy of 3, both to protect against foolishly losing your temper, as well as to protect against others unleashing their anger on you.

It is always beneficial to be mindful of the number 3 star, and to make sure the correct remedies are put in place at the center of your home or room. Wearing gold (which signifies Metal) is an excellent way to stay personally protected, especially if you wear **chrome gold protective amulets.** But better yet when there is the strong presence of the colour red to signify the presence of Fire energy. Fire exhausts the Wood element of the number 3, while simultaneously strengthening your Earth element. The colour red is therefore doubly beneficial to the Dog. In 2015, it is a good idea for the Dog to strengthen Fire element energy around you. You can do this with **bright lights** or a red colour scheme in your interior decor using **yang red scatter cushions**.

CURES FOR THE #3: The best remedy for the number 3 star is the symbolic representation of the **7 Royal Emblems** etched on chrome gold and embedded against a red plaque that symbolizes the presence of the Fire element. This combination of Fire with Metal energy makes the remedy very strong indeed, although usually, anything that is red in colour – a wall, a door, or a red carpet or red curtains, even nine red stones, can be effective as a remedy to subdue the number 3 star.

Incorporating the 7 royal emblems is extremely auspicious. These emblems include the Dharmachakra Wheel in the center surrounded by images of the Precious Queen symbolizing the all-important matriarchal energy, the Precious Minister to look after all domestic affairs, the Precious General for protection. These images are placed above. Below there is the Precious Jewel to symbolize the wish-fulfilling gemstone, the Precious Horse to signify success and the Precious Elephant to represent power. The red background ensures harmony in the home.

This specially designed cure symbolizes a well-managed and happy home that nurtures the whole family. These emblems are borrowed from the Tibetan Cosmic feng shui texts. They bring enormous good fortune when placed at the center of any home.

As a secondary remedy, which you can use for the important rooms of the home such as bedrooms, family rooms and dining rooms, hang the **bright red 9 Amulet Plaque** cure with **powerful Anti-Hostility Amulet.** This will protect household members from becoming victims of petty people with bad tempers. It also prevents aggravating energies causing you and your family to suffer from other people's temper tantrums, unreasonable behaviour or road rage.

MAHABOUDI STUPA
FOR SPIRITUAL PROTECTION

Because of the number 3 star in the center of this year's chart, we decided to create something really special, so we are thrilled to bring to our readers this **incredible replica of the mighty Mahaboudi Stupa**, which I was inspired to create after two successful Pilgrimages I led to this most holy place in India with my friends and students.

We went to the village of Bodhgaya where the historical **Buddha Shakyamuni** attained Enlightenment meditating under the legendary Bodhi tree and on this holy site, this fabulous Stupa has been built. It is a place where millions come each year to benefit from the spiritual aura that hovers so peacefully over the grounds of the entire complex.

This Stupa has been filled with thousands of printed paper mantras, with some in microfilm to increase their numbers inside. These are **secret mantras** placed inside the stupa and this together with the exquisite workmanship embellished with "jewels" make this Stupa extremely blessed.

We feel very fortunate to have the karma, the resources and the contacts to do this. That we are able to offer this special Stupa at our stores and online eCommerce site is something we value very much. We do not aim to make profit from these Stupas. More than anything, we designed these to create spiritual merit and to share the wonderful benefits of doing so. Please note that inviting this Stupa into your home and placing it in the center if you can will completely remove all the "poisons" that afflict households.

You will observe that after you bring this Stupa into your home, there will be fewer conflict

moments, less aggravations… and a lot more loving, peaceful feelings generated. The Stupa will help keep bad influences and bad people from infiltrating your home. It is really very beneficial, and if you **offer flowers, water bowls or lights to the Stupa daily**, it will cause your spiritual strength to grow and expand. And all these benefits will occur slowly without you even noticing. One day, you simply wake up to the realization that it has happened and you realize you are feeling a lot happier and less stressed.

BASIC GUIDELINES ON ACTIVATING ENERGY

Please note that lucky and unlucky numbers usually manifest their effects when they get energized, so a good rule to follow is wherever sectors are afflicted by the bad numbers bringing bad luck, those sectors are best kept quiet. No noisy renovations, no TV sets and definitely you must reduce noise levels.

In 2015 when the number 3 star is in the center, it is advisable to keep the center of your home peaceful and quiet.

Not a good idea to have too many people sitting there activating the 3, or having the TV or radio at full blast. Try to keep the center of your home undisturbed and move all socializing to another sector of your home.

> ***NO DIGGING IN THE WEST & SOUTHWEST:*** In the garden make sure there is no digging, no cutting of trees and no construction in those sectors that are afflicted i.e. in the center of the garden, in the West corner of the garden and also the Southwest of the garden where the *Tai Sui* or God of the Year of 2015 resides.

Those living in apartments must note what is taking place within view of their apartment. When there is construction work going on within view in the sector directions that are afflicted, please use a curtain to shut out the view! For sectors where lucky numbers have flown to however, it is excellent to move the energy with lots of noisy activity. Have the **radio or TV or a fan** placed

here to churn up the energy so there is a good noise level. Also install **brighter lights**. Moving the energy in these three ways will encourage yang chi to manifest to your advantage.

In 2015, the **three luckiest sectors** are **North, East** and **Northeast,** which play host to the numbers 8, 1 and 6 stars respectively.

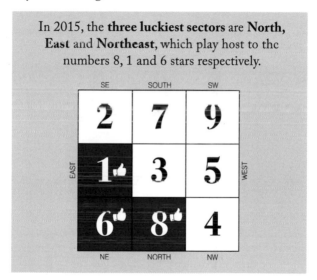

STAR OF ROMANCE IN THE NORTHWEST

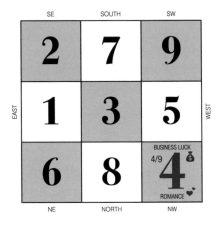

The number 4 *Romance Star* flies to the Northwest in 2015, **bringing love and romance to the Dog sign,** but also perhaps unwelcome distractions to the Patriarchs and leaders of the world. Those amongst the male movers and shakers of the world are likely to be more focused on achieving enhanced economic gains than on love and romance; although because the number 4 brings the *Peach Blossom Star,* circumstances could develop that may distract the Patriarchal figure as well as those residing in the Northwest sector of their homes. There can be romantic dalliances, but because the year is well-balanced, it is unlikely for romantic entanglements to cause too much scandal.

But because it is in the Northwest of the chart, here we see the Metal energy of the Northwest suppressing the strength of the 4 Wood star. From this, we can surmise that 2015 is a year when romantic indulgences will be clear-headed.

> The number 4 star on its own has little real strength. Usually, the number 4 also brings great education luck in addition to a particular focus on marriage. But to a large extent, both of these kinds of luck need to be strongly self-generated. These two categories of luck thus depend as much on individual fortunes.

Those keen on manifesting romance luck will need to work a lot harder. If you are single and looking to find a love partner this year, our advice is to enhance this sector of your bedroom or living room with a potent love energizer featuring the **Double Happiness emblem with a pair of Mandarin Ducks.**

Instead, what will engage your interest will be your business concerns. Patriarchs and leaders, CEO's and the men who are in charge of corporations should take advantage of the lucky *Earth Seal* 24 mountain star and *Ho Tu* combination created in the Northwest by the annual number 4 star with the Period number 9. This creates the *Ho Tu* of 4/9, which brings awesome business luck to the sector benefiting Patriarchs. **The Dog also benefits in the same way.**

HO TU ENHANCERS: Ho Tu numbers are always best activated with brass mirrors and it is a good idea for men to place a 4/9 enhancing Ho Tu mirror on your desk in the Northwest corner. For everyone whose important rooms and/or bedroom are located in the Northwest, will benefit from carrying a **4/9 Ho Tu mirror** with you wherever you go.

SAFEGUARDING THE WEST
Suppressing the misfortune star 5
to protect rooms and doors in the West

This year, those whose homes face or sit West, and whose main doors are located in their West sector are negatively affected by the *wu wang*, ie the Five Yellow, a major misfortune star. Its location in the West also

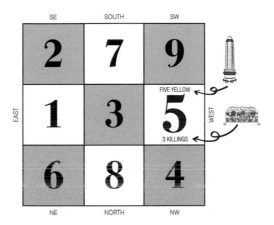

afflicts the **young women** of the household – usually this refers to the youngest daughter, to second wives and to the young women of households. It is a good idea to move out of any West-located room this year to avoid the ill effects of the *wu wang*, because it is such a nasty star! The West is a Metal sector and this makes it strong enough to exhaust the potency of the 5, thereby making the *Five Yellow* less dangerous. Unfortunately, the Period 8 number of the West is 1, which is Water, and the Earth energy of number 5 easily overcomes the intrinsic energy of 1. Since all the numbers in this sector are clashing, the energy yin in the West is quite afflicted this year, and thus strong cures should be placed to control the energies here.

THE HEART SUTRA PILLAR

The remedy used for suppressing the number 5 this year must have the appearance of Strong Metal, hence we have created an awesome pillar etched with the Heart Sutra, a powerful sacred sutra that will keep the 5 under control. The 5 must be suppressed in a way which makes it unable to harm the rest of the household.

Note that the West is also afflicted by the *Natural Disaster Star* brought by the 24 Mountains. In fact, the West is quite badly afflicted in 2015, hence the use of this sacred pillar as a cure. It has a lotus base and a strong mount above – these together with the sutra etched on the pillar will absorb all the afflictive energies in the West sector this year. Place the **Heart Sutra Pillar** brightly chromed in gold as a cure against the Five Yellow. This can be the main remedy for the number 5 star this year. Its presence in the home will also enhance the secondary cures used to suppress the number 5 star in the other rooms of the house, as well as those you carry with you. The Heart Sutra Pillar can be displayed in any room occupied by you that is located in the West.

BEWARE APRIL, JULY, & JANUARY (2016)

You must also be extra careful when the monthly number 5 travels to this sector as that is when the *wu wang* gets doubled. This happens in April 2015 and January 2016. It is important to be extra careful against illness during the month of July, as this is when the illness star joins forces with the *wu wang*. This same advice is extended to those whose main doors are located in the West sector of their homes

REMEDIES FOR THE WEST

1 The best remedy then is the **Heart Sutra Sacred Pillar**. This can also be viewed as a powerful holy object which can completely subdue the malevolent energy of the 5 star. It has the power to bring local spirit protectors to your side. Placing the Heart Sutra itself is already an excellent safeguard against bad people, illness, accidents and reversals of fortunes.

2 Another magnificent cure to complement the power of the Sacred Pillar is the **5-Spoked Thunderbolt** which you can use as an additional cure for the *Wu Wang* especially during months when the 2 or 5 flies into this secot. This Strong Metal instrument is believed to possess spiritual cosmic powers that are strong enough to suppress the number 5 in a way that makes it unable to harm the rest of the household. The 5-spoked thunderbolt, also known as the vajra is a powerful symbol of indestructability which Buddhists believe to be the main implement of the famed Guru Rinpoche.

The 5-spoked Thunderbolt suppresses the Five Yellow affliction.

THREE KILLINGS IN THE WEST
Overcoming three poisonous harmful winds

In 2015, the West suffers from the poisonous winds of the Three Killings. It afflicts all homes that face or have main doors located in the West. The Three Killings bring the potential for three kinds of losses – loss of wealth, loss of good name and loss of a loved one. It should not be "disturbed" and we recommend against undertaking any kind of renovations in the West sector of your home or office.

CURE FOR THE THREE KILLINGS: For 2015, we recommend suppressing this with the **Three Celestial Guardians Five Element Yang Metal Cure**. This is a specially made small metal container that has three large coloured glass crystals in yellow, blue and green to signify Earth, Water and Wood set in them. A small candle tea light is placed within to awaken the Fire element.

When the candle is lit, it wakes up the five elements. This is a powerful way to suppress the Three Killings, but it is not easy to find such a cure. We decided to manufacture this cure for placement in the West, as the *wu wang* also being in the West makes it a very badly afflicted sector this year. To engage the assistance of the three celestial guardians, we have also incorporated these wonderful protector guardians into the design. Light the candle inside the container to symbolize **Yang Fire** to overcome and exhaust the Three Killings.

It is only Fire energy that can suppress the Three Killings in a Metal sector. This cure is especially suitable for safeguarding the feng shui of you work desk and office. Place it on a side board or table in the West corner of your office.

SUPPRESSING THE ILLNESS STAR 2 IN THE SOUTHEAST
Protecting the eldest daughter against severe illness afflictions

The number 2 illness star is in the Southeast sector where it meets the Period number of 7. This reduces its severity and can even transform number 2 star into a potentially lucrative source of **big money luck**. This is because the 7 star is Metal, thus it exhausts the Earth energy of the number 2. Note that the number 2 when combined with the Period star 7 creates the *Ho Tu* combination of 2/7, which brings big money luck. Nevertheless, bedrooms or doors located here in the Southeast can still be affected by illness energy. It is advisable to keep this part of your house quiet.

Excessive activity here can agitate the illness star. Bright lights are not advisable. The illness star is an Earth element star, and Fire energy strengthens it.

CURES FOR THE NUMBER 2: If you are worried about the illness star because you are already ill as you read this, or your bedroom is located in the Southeast corner of your home, we suggest a Taoist or Buddhist remedy. There is no harm in placing both types of remedies, as one is a worldly cure and the other a cosmic spiritual cure.

1 MEDICINE BUDDHA MANDALA PLAQUE showing the curative herbs and healing substances. Hanging this in the Southeast strengthens the Wood element of the Southeast while powerful invocations to the Medicine Buddha ensures fast recovery for those who are ill.

You can also get the **Medicine Buddha Plaque** which contains the names of the 8 Medicine Buddhas (referred to as the 8 Sugata brothers) with the powerful healing mantra. Hang this plaque on the Southeast wall in 2015 to keep the illness star subdued.

2 A strong Taoist remedy against illness is the symbolic **Golden Wu Lou**, especially one that has been imprinted with the image of the mythical **Garuda Bird**. The Wu Lou itself is already a very strong suppresser of the number 2 star but when it is guarded by the Garuda, it provides even stronger protection against illness. This is because the Garuda bird is regarded as the only creature that can subdue *naga spirits* that cause cancer, skin disorders and lung problems. When placed in the Southeast, the **Garuda Wu Lou** will keep illness vibes well under control.

3 Finally, one of the most powerful spiritual cures against illness is to invite the presence of the Buddha known as **Orgyen Menla**. Orgyen Menla has the power to completely vanquish *all illnesses* brought by astrological afflictions and spirit attacks. He embodies all the healing qualities of Medicine Buddha and Guru Rinpoche combined. Orgyen Menla can be placed on your altar or anywhere in your home that is elevated and respectful.

CURE FOR THE DANGEROUS 7 IN THE SOUTH
Protecting the household against burglary and robbery

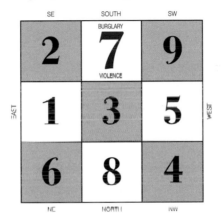

In this Year of the Sheep, the strong violent and negative vibes associated with burglary seem to have subsided and home security is not as dangerous an issue as it was in the previous two years. Nevertheless, it is still beneficial to stay safeguarded against the danger of the number 7 star, which brings burglary and robbery afflictions. The number 7 is a **Metal star** that is red in colour, and 7 is always equated with blood. Its symbolic association is the "injured soldier".

Hence this number is usually associated with armed robbery and violence. In 2015, it flies to the South, a Fire sector. This weakens the 7, because Fire destroys Metal, and hence the 7 star is not as strong as it was in the previous year.

If your main door faces South, your home is also afflicted by the 7 and if your bedroom is situated in the South corner of your home the number 7 can also harm you. It is a good idea to subdue this star where it occurs.

CURES FOR THE VIOLENT 7:

1 It is easier to suppress the number 7 star this year because it is weak, and if you strengthen the Fire energies in the South part of the home, it should be very effective in warding off the negativities of the 7 star. The thing to do then is to **enhance the brightness** of your lights in this sector. This should be a sufficiently good cure.

2 Nevertheless, for those who want to be doubly sure, you can place traditional **Door**

Guardians in this part of the home. It is always beneficial to have a pair of **Elephants** or **Rhinos** or other door guardians that take your fancy placed flanking your main door. These help keep unwanted visitors from

getting into your home. Symbolic door guardians do not just keep robbers from disturbing your sleep at nights; they also ensure that people who pretend to be your friends and who harbour secret negative thoughts about you are also kept away. Good feng shui always safeguards you against people who have bad intentions towards you. Anyone who bring aggravations and problems into your life cannot get to you.

3 If your bedroom is located in the South or any of your household members are born in the year of the Horse, then it is necessary to protect this corner of the home with the **Anti-Burglary Totem** as this will keep any violent vibes from causing them harm. The Anti-Burglary Totem should also be placed in the South when the monthly 7 visits.

STAR OF FUTURE PROSPERITY IN THE SOUTHWEST
Energizing the number 9 is becoming increasingly effective

As we move strongly into the second decade of this 21st century, we get unrelentingly closer to the final period of this age as we draw closer to entering the new period of 9. This happens in 2024. The number 9 signifies a **new age of prosperity** and the influence of the number is getting stronger each year.

In 2015, the number 9 flies to the Southwest, the sector of the matriarch.

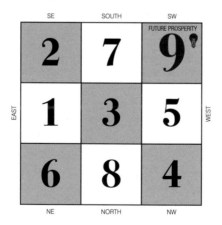

This is excellent news as anything that benefits the matriarch usually benefits the whole household. The number 9 is a gloriously magnifying star and it enhances the hidden strengths of women in the shaping of the world's fortunes, influencing our collective consciousness and bringing new awareness of the enhanced public role being played by women.

If you are a woman competing within a corporate or political environment, your gender gives you an added advantage over your male colleagues this year.

It is no coincidence that there are presently many influential and powerful women occupying key global strategic positions. Women are running the governments of many countries so it is very auspicious for them that the all-powerful *Star of Future Prosperity* has flown into the Southwest.

There is a strengthening of the energy in this part of the home. With the 9 here in 2015 and the number 8 coming in 2016, female authoritative power will continue to advance in the coming two years. If the main door is located in or facing the Southwest, or the bedroom is in the Southwest, it benefits the mother or the older women of the household to strongly energize this sector of the home.

Enhance the **Fire element energy** of this sector. Do this for all your important rooms and for the whole house – bring in a **red carpet**, paint the wall red, hang **red coloured curtains** and use **red cushions.**

The colour red will strongly enhance the numbers 8 as well as 9. All red-coloured furnishings in the Southwest will thus be good feng shui for the next two years. It will strengthen the *mother energy* of the home benefiting everyone in the household.

ENHANCER FOR THE SOUTHWEST:
Look for the **9 Red Peacock** or **9 Red Phoenix Tapestry** to place in the Southwest of your home. This is a potent enhancer for the number 9 as it is associated with these kings of birds, and according to whether you prefer the peacocks (which stand for success and recognition) or the phoenix (which

are powerful symbols of love and prosperity), you can display either of these fabulous feathered creatures.

Birds suggest the soaring ability of taking flight and having 9 of them covers the full spectrum of collective combinations. This is a numerology thing, because 9 is a number that represents the fullness of the Universe. Everything starts and ends with the number 9. Indeed, the number 9 multiplied by whatever number always results in digits that add up once again to 9. When we display nine auspicious birds, we are thus capturing the full spectrum of the luck we want in all its favourable manifestations.

The peacock/phoenix tapestries must contain the sun and the moon in the skies, as well as show rocks and trees on the ground to signify the cosmic manifestations of great good fortune that bring not just *current* but also *future* prosperity. We have made these screens for your Southwest walls. You can also get them in miniature to be placed in the Southwest corner of your office to bring you good fortune for the coming two years. Display them as prominently as you can and **shine a bright light** to awaken their cosmic energy. Birds bring new prosperity and new opportunities. Their images are very lucky to have inside the home.

THE NORTHEAST BENEFITS FROM THE STAR OF 6
White number brings strong divine luck

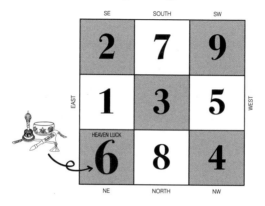

In 2015, the number 6 flies to the Northeast, bringing courage and confidence to households facing or sitting Northeast. This is a *Big Metal* number flying into an Earth sector, so it could also bring exhaustion to the young men of the family. Note that the number 6 possesses strong Patriarchal energy, so young men of the household will tend to get pressured by the family patriarch. The 6 in the Northeast brings with it expectations that can cause tensions and family conflicts between father and sons. Usually, we activate this auspicious star number (because it is auspicious) with beautiful metallic windchimes, but **in 2015, it is**

better to use *yin* rather than yang metallic enhancers. There should not be excessive heavy metal sound, as this will cause tensions to get heightened. A gentle kind of humming sound created by **singing bells or bowls** are much better for enhancing the positive energies of the number 6 star.

ENHANCER FOR THE #6: The key to getting the best out of the number 6 is to strengthen the Earth energy of the Northeast. This is because Earth creates Metal, so placing **six crystal enhancers** here is a good way to bring good fortune to this sector of the home. We designed a **crystal ball globe flanked by the Tiger and Ox** to strengthen the energy of the NE. Placing this powerful enhancer here with **six smaller crystals** will hype up the cosmic energy of the entire household. It will also benefit the younger men and sons of the family, bringing them unexpected good fortune luck.

ENERGIZING 8 IN THE NORTH
Strengthening wealth luck with earth energy

In 2015, the wealth-bringing number 8 star flies to the North. Here the number 8 brings very **auspicious winds** to the household, especially if there is a strong

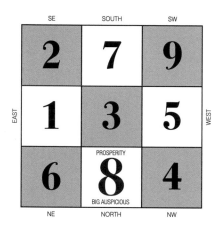

	SE	SOUTH	SW	
EAST	**2**	**7**	**9**	
	1	**3**	**5**	WEST
	6	PROSPERITY **8** BIG AUSPICIOUS	**4**	
	NE	NORTH	NW	

presence of water here. The number 8 is a strong number.

In the North, its **Earth element** controls this **Water sector**. The 8 star in 2015 benefits those whose bedrooms or whose homes have main doors located in their North. Those occupying a room in this sector should strengthen Earth and Water energy in their North corners by hanging an **8-rod crystal windchime containing the symbols of water droplets.** The crystal windchime will create plenty of suitable Earth music to empower the 8, while the small crystal water droplets will attract abundance for the occupants.

NOTE: These special crystal windchimes work very well for energizing Earth stars, so they must **NOT** be hung in sectors afflicted by the Earth 5 and Earth 2 stars, otherwise they can bring misfortune instead of good fortune.

Usually, when we hang windchimes, whether metallic or crystal, it is really important to be very exact when it comes to their placement; otherwise they can bring unwanted developments and bad luck instead of bringing good fortune.

It is also important to remove them when you update your feng shui at year end. In fact, for ALL the cures and enhancers, you MUST be mindful about removing last year's cures, and replace them with a new set of cures. Thus please hang these crystal windchimes in the North sectors of your home only in 2015.

MONGOOSE SPOUTING JEWELS

Prosperity luck for the whole house can be created by energizing the 8 in the North with a mongoose spouting gold placed here. The presence of a mongoose is always a powerful way to activate for a good flow of wealth luck because the mongoose is a powerful cosmic symbol of wealth. It is popular amongst many of the Asian cultural traditions as a bringer of prosperity; it ensures that families graced by its symbolic presence never suffer from a shortage of food and sustenance, will never suffer from poverty.

This is because the mongoose belongs to the Rat family and the Rat is legendary in its ability to never go hungry. Of the twelve signs, the Rat is the most efficient at making a good living under any circumstance. The mongoose does not bring direct wealth. What it does is spew forth from its mouth a vast array of wishfulfilling gems and jewels. **Thus it brings to you whatever you wish for!**

But you must get your mind involved in this cure, because you need to actively wish for the kind of prosperity you want. <u>Give an image to your wishes</u> - perhaps a new house, a car, a special luxury you have always wanted or even a new business idea.

Everyone can benefit from this year's location of 8 by using this powerful enhancer to bring you good potential for prosperity. Not many are aware that all the wonderful symbols placed in homes to manifest a variety of good fortune work best when there is smooth cosmic alignment between our thoughts and these images. Feng shui always brings spectacular results when the connectivity between the human consciousnesses of the household is fully in sync with the symbolic ornaments that are placed within.

ENERGIZING 1 IN THE EAST
Strengthening growth & victory for the household

SE	SOUTH	SW
2	7	9
VICTORY 1 (EAST)	3	5 (WEST)
6	8	4
NE	NORTH	NW

The East sector in all buildings benefit from the presence of the powerful **number 1 Victory Star,** which brings good fortune and quick success luck. This star is especially beneficial for those whose homes face or sit East.

If your bedroom or main door is located in your East sector, you can enjoy the luck of this white number. Yang Water will awaken the benefits of the number 1 star in the East sector. The element here is Wood which gets strengthened when there is Water. Having a **pond** or a **pool** here is very beneficial and is something to seriously consider if you are building your dream house this year. Creating water in the East sector is always beneficial for attracting big wealth. A pool of water here brings prosperity wealth to the household. You can accumulate **asset wealth** here and **business luck** will also be very good.

The Lotus and Carp feature activates the Victory 1 and attracts abundance year after year. Place it in the East in 2015.

CHAPTER 3
THE 24 MOUNTAINS AND THE HO TUS OF 2015

THE 24 MOUNTAINS STARS OF 2015

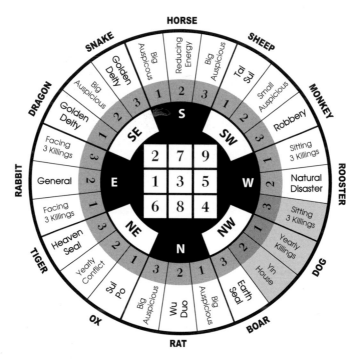

This year's astrology compass of annual stars of the
24 Mountains reveal a lot fewer conflict stars than
in previous years, so generally it can be said that this
year, there should be less aggressive behaviour than in

the previous year. Last year, this same compass wheel and other charts indicated a very rough Horse Year that was also unbalanced, so in both East and West hemispheres of the world, we came close to the kind of confrontation between countries that could have led to war. It appears that this year, conflict energy recedes...

DOG HAS SOME YIN AFFLICTIONS

The 24 Mountains stars bring extra dimensions to the fortunes of animal signs, so it is a good thing that in this Year of the Sheep, there are more auspicious stars than in the previous year and less conflict indications. Unfortunately, the Dog's location does not seem to be benefitting from lucky stars. Instead, the Dog sign is afflicted by *Yearly Killing* and *Three Killing* stars, as well as having close proximity to the star of the *Yin House.*

What this means is that you have to endure the *yin energies* brought by three significant stars of the 24 Mountains. These generally bring challenges when even one such star appears next to your sign, but to have one on each side, and to also be playing host to the *Yearly Killing Star* can be very trying.

The Dog is thus afflicted by the stars of the 24 Mountains in 2015. It is very beneficial in your situation then to **install the remedies** that can subdue these afflictive stars, so that whatever negatives they may be bringing with them gets reduced or is dissolved completely. Otherwise, some big misfortune could well manifest for you in 2015 that can prove traumatic. What you need to do is to place powerful cures that cause the killing luck stars to be subdued; best would be the presence of the **Three Celestial Guardians**, the Chi Lin, the Fu Dog and the Pi Yao.

But it is also necessary for the Dog to try and benefit from the good fortune stars of the 24 Mountains. Hence you need to examine the influence of the other 24 Mountain stars on the luck of your home. Remember that all sectors of the 24 Mountains compass exert their influence on all houses and offices.

Firstly note that both the **North** and **South** sectors of all homes are flanked by *Big Auspicious Stars*, which bring great good fortune for those whose homes are oriented North/South, or whose bedrooms are located in either of these sectors in the home. These are East group directions that benefit those of you born under the **East group Kua numbers**.

Another sector that enjoys similar good direction is the Southeast 3 direction. If your house is facing or sitting in this direction, you too are flanked by *Stars of Big Auspicious*. These extremely powerful stars indicate that something significant and meaningful can actualize in a favourable way for residents of the houschold with doors facing Southeast.

The 24 mountain stars exert similar influences on the animal signs whose home location (see Astrology Compass) directly benefit from being flanked by these stars.

NORTH & SOUTH
Big Auspicious Luck All Round

The North and South locations benefit from good fortune stars, but these sectors **need to be activated** to manifest the favourable results brought by nearby auspicious stars.

Try to **strengthen the South** with Fire element enhancers that activate the element of the South, keeping the burglary affliction here under control and giving a strong boost to the *Big Auspicious stars*. Excellent additional placements to magnify the luck of the South is to display **red carpets** or **cushions** here. Increase the **brightness of your lighting** in this sector

2015 STARS OF THE 24 MOUNTAINS
SOUTH
SOUTH 1: Big Auspicious **SOUTH 2:** Reducing Energy **SOUTH 3:** Big Auspicious

Place red carpets, red pillows, tangerines & pears and bright lights in the SOUTH to manifest BIG AUSPICIOUS for the whole house.

and display auspicious symbols i.e. tangerine oranges and pears to simulate "big luck coming" (*tai kat tai lay*).. These yang boosting enhancers will ensure that the *Big Auspicious Stars* will manifest to benefit your household. Family members who belong to the sign of the Horse benefit the most from these feng shui enhancements as the South is the home location of the Horse. Remember that when you improve your time dimension feng shui each new year, you are benefitting other members of your household as well.

You should do the same for your **North sector** as here too there are two *Big Auspicious Stars,* which must be activated to bring members of the household a big inflow of good fortune. This can actualize as a new job offer or an elevated position, which brings more authority and added income streams for the father or mother. It can also actualize as a sudden windfall of money.

The stars in the North benefit family members born in the year of the Rat.

For the North, you can boost the strength of the stars by having the presence of Water. If possible, display the **Inukshuk Water Feature** to create positive yang water vibrations. If this is difficult, then at the very least, display a **decorative vase or bowl** containing water placed in this corner. Use transparent glass containers made of crystal or glass. They should not be

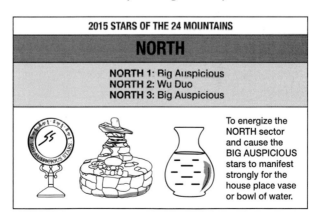

2015 STARS OF THE 24 MOUNTAINS

NORTH

NORTH 1: Big Auspicious
NORTH 2: Wu Duo
NORTH 3: Big Auspicious

To energize the NORTH sector and cause the BIG AUSPICIOUS stars to manifest strongly for the house place vase or bowl of water.

too small and preferably have a larger opening and a neck to resemble the traditional vase shape.

The key here is to give the water **as large a surface area as possible**. We have been placing big bowls of water in every corner that benefits from the Water element for many years now. Our dogs live indoors with the family and quench their thirst from the water bowls, which are quite big and placed on the floor.

Change the water each morning; this way, the water bowls meant for energizing auspicious stars not only have a feng shui benefit, they also serve to ensure enough saturation of the thirst of your pets, who are of course a great source of *yang chi* for the house. The presence of water will energize the *Big Auspicious* stars here to actualize good fortune for the household.

SOUTHEAST
A Trio of Good Fortune

The Southeast direction and location enjoys a trio of excellent good fortune stars, benefiting all homes facing or sitting Southeast or that have bedrooms or main doors in this sector. If you live in a house like this, **energize the door with plenty of usage** and also enhance the Southeast with a **strong presence of Wood** energy.

This makes the sector itself strong and vigourous, and creates the kind of ambience that will cause the auspicious stars here to bring your household both worldly and spiritual good fortune. The beneficial stars of the Southeast brought by the 24 Mountains are the *Star of Big Auspicious* flanked by two stars of *Golden Deity*, with each of the latter stars sitting in the **Dragon** and **Snake** home locations. This benefits those born under these signs.

Having a bedroom or workroom here for example means you can benefit from these lucky stars. The best placements for the Southeast are potted plants, especially those that are in bloom. This is because Southeast is activated by the Wood element. It also

---

2015 STARS OF THE 24 MOUNTAINS

SOUTHEAST

SOUTHEAST 1: Golden Deity
SOUTHEAST 2: Big Auspicious
SOUTHEAST 3: Golden Deity

To energize the SOUTHEAST & GOLDEN DEITY stars to manifest strongly for the house, place images of deities.

signifies the **eldest daughter** of the family, who will also benefit from fresh flowers being placed here. **Plants with fresh flowers** are considered the best enhancers for this direction whenever auspicious stars fly into the space.

It is also good feng shui to have placements of **Golden Deities** here to activate their positive star indications. Golden Deities can be from any spiritual tradition or religion. Their presence is usually enough to trigger the auspicious blessings brought by the Deities, but if you have an altar with consecrated Deities inside your home, they will automatically cause the *Star of Golden Deity* to get activated. It is not necessary to invite any new deity into the home, although once again, if you do so, there is an added benefit. This is the way placement feng shui works. The addition of new decorative pieces into the home always brings fresh new vigour to the home environment.

ACTIVATING BIG AUSPICIOUS

Note that for all three directions, **South, North** and **Southeast,** you should ensure that the *Star of Big Auspicious* is activated to bring significant improvement to your status. This is best done by having a **brass mirror** or **grand bejewelled throne** at the front of the house near the entrance. This should reflect in big auspicious luck, as this star **occurs five times** in the 24 Mountains this year. Another way to attract *Big Auspicious* luck to manifest - what the Chinese refer to proverbially as *'Tai Kat Tai Lay'* - refers to the placement of **succulent tangerine oranges** and **golden pears** near sectors where *Big Auspicious Stars* are located. These need not be real oranges and pears, but during the fifteen days of the lunar new year especially, do display oranges and pears in these sectors to pull in big auspicious luck.

NORTHWEST
Benefitting from the Earth Seal

The Northwest has the powerful *Star of Earth Seal*, which brings a grounding energy that is extremely beneficial for the Patriarch and his family. All that is needed to strengthen this star is to have a **plate-full of coloured stones.** Get **smooth river stones** and paint them with the **colours of the earth,** ranging from **reds**

2015 STARS OF THE 24 MOUNTAINS
NORTHWEST

NORTHWEST 1: Year Killing
NORTHWEST 2: Yin House
NORTHWEST 3: Earth Seal

For the NORTHWEST
- Strengthen EARTH SEAL with stones
- Suppress YEAR KILLING with magic wheel
- Suppress YIN HOUSE with yang house

to hues of **yellows** and **orange**. The presence of these stones enhances the chi of Earth, which strengthens the sector's energy, bringing good feng shui.

The Northwest also plays host to negative stars of *Yin House* and *Year Killing*, which must be dealt with. The idea is to change their frequency from bad to positive by placing symbolic remedies in this sector. Create an image of a "**yang house**" either as a wall print or as a painting. Yin houses are for the dead, while yang houses are for the living. At its most extreme, *Yin House* indicates a death in the family, but with the remedy suggested, you create a countering force, so any negative impact of this affliction can be averted.

It is important to check if the man of the house is suffering from any kind of illness or experiencing low life force; if so, it is a good idea not to stay in a room in the Northwest

For the Dog, note that you enjoy a good life force so the *Yin House syndrome* should not cause you personally a serious problem. What the Dog needs to be guarded against is the *Star of Year Killing*, which can be a harmful indication that can cause serious rifts amongst family members that lead to tragic situations. Do take note of this and suppress the effect of this star with the talisman we call the **Magic Wheel**. This is a house amulet and it is the image of a wheel with eight spokes symbolizing eight spiritual protectors.

You can look on this as a Protection Wheel as there is a powerful mantra circling the wheel; in the center of the wheel is the protective syllable Hum. Placed in the Northwest, the Magic Wheel offers the Patriarch (or male relative if any) powerful protection from unscrupulous people as well as potential spirit harm. With the conflict star brought by the number 3 in the center of the 2015 feng shui chart, protecting the Northwest sector this way is an important safeguard for the family's well being.

WEST
Very afflicted in 2015

The sector of the West direction is very afflicted this year as it plays host to the *Three Killings* as well as the *Natural Disaster Star*. These afflictions can cause a variety of ills that can change your life and cause you much grief. It is really important to suppress the impact of these stars and to make sure you are strong enough to avoid the consequences of their presence in the West. Those of you who have missing West sectors have no cause to worry, but if your bedroom or main door is placed in the West, then you might well fall foul of these stars and suffer some misfortune. The same can be said for those of you whose homes sit West (i.e. facing East.) The *Three Killings* bring three

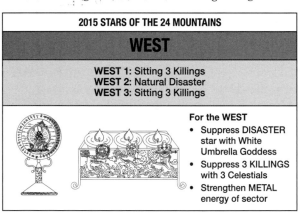

2015 STARS OF THE 24 MOUNTAINS

WEST

WEST 1: Sitting 3 Killings
WEST 2: Natural Disaster
WEST 3: Sitting 3 Killings

For the WEST
- Suppress DISASTER star with White Umbrella Goddess
- Suppress 3 KILLINGS with 3 Celestials
- Strengthen METAL energy of sector

kinds of bad luck that have to do with loss of wealth, loss of your good name and loss of a loved one. These kinds of misfortune are severe when they affect you, either directly or indirectly.

This afflictive star in West 3 affects the Dog sign indirectly.

The good news is that this star is not difficult to neutralize. What you need are all three of the **Celestial Guardians** so popular with the Chinese for so many centuries. These are the Fu Dog, the Pi Yao and the Chi Lin.

The **Fu Dog** is a popular door guardian widely used by the Imperial family. You can see many Fu Dogs in the Forbidden City and around Beijing. The **Pi Yao** comes with horns and resembles the snow lion. The Pi Yao is extremely popular with the people of Shanghai and amongst many old cities of the Himalayan valleys. There are many Pi Yaos in many of the temples of Nepal. This creature is considered necessary for guarding all premises, especially for those involved with the armed forces or those doing business. The **Chi Lin** is a legendary creature described as a combination of the mythical Dragon and the Horse. It combines the courage of the Horse with the power of the Dragon.

With the presence of all three **Celestial Guardians** in the West, the *Three Killings Star* becomes totally subdued. If you add a statue of **Ksiddhigarba** to the three celestials, the protective aura increases many times over.

Meanwhile, to overcome the *Disaster Star,* engage the power of the **White Umbrella Goddess.** You can do this by displaying the plaque enhanced with the image and invocations of the Goddess together with her all powerful seed syllable "OM".

The White Umbrella Goddess deflects off the impact of extreme weather that brings natural disasters; it also protects against misfortune brought by extreme winds, big fires, angry waters and shifting earth. When you think about it, these are exactly what cause natural disasters, and these are the four elements of the cosmic realms.

The **White Umbrella Goddess** who is all-powerful at dispersing all misfortune including dangers brought by magic diagrams and bad spells. It is beneficial to strengthen the Metal chi energy of the West sector.

EAST
Facing the Three Killings

The East sector has the affliction "facing the Three Killings" although it is interesting to note that any direct confrontation with the Three Killings does not harm you. You can sit facing West and not be afflicted. Nevertheless, it is safer to place the same **Three Celestials** here in the East, especially if your bedroom or main door is located here.

The East is a Wood sector, which represents the eldest son of the family, so it is worthwhile putting remedies here. To strengthen the chi energy of this sector, place **Bejewelled Tree** here. In 2015, it is beneficial to do so, as this brings out all the best attributes of this

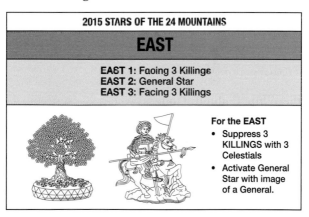

2015 STARS OF THE 24 MOUNTAINS

EAST

EAST 1: Facing 3 Killings
EAST 2: General Star
EAST 3: Facing 3 Killings

For the EAST
- Suppress 3 KILLINGS with 3 Celestials
- Activate General Star with image of a General.

direction. The Bejewelled Tree with lots of "jewels" hanging off the tree brings excellent growth chi to the East.

SOUTHWEST
Benefits from the Tai Sui

The Southwest in 2015 benefits from the support of the *Tai Sui*, the God of the Year, who moves around the compass from year to year and is always located in the direction of the animal sign that rules the year. This year it occupies the Sheep location of Southwest 1.

Always remember that you must not confront the Tai Sui. In 2015, this means do not sit directly facing

---

2015 STARS OF THE 24 MOUNTAINS

SOUTHWEST

SOUTHWEST 1: Tai Sui
SOUTHWEST 2: Small Auspicious
SOUTHWEST 3: Robbery

For the SOUTHWEST
- Activate SMALL AUSPICIOUS
- Appease TAI SUI with Amulet
- Suppress ROBBERY star

SW1; observe this taboo even if this is one of your favourable directions.

Refrain from making excessive noise in the Southwest 1 sector. Do not undertake renovation or allow any digging, cutting or demolition works to be done here. Breaking this taboo can bring sudden and severe misfortune to befall the household. It can cause surrounding cosmic spirits to get out of sync and start disturbing your household. Any sudden haunting is usually caused by someone in the household inadvertently offending this God of the Year. Appease the *Tai Sui* by placing the year's **Tai Sui amulet** here.

> Note that the *Tai Sui* persona **changes each year**, hence the need for a **new amulet plaque** each year.

In Southwest 2 is the *Star of Small Auspicious* and this benefits the Monkey. While this may not bring as spectacular a benefit as its big counterpart, nevertheless, this star brings a sustained series of good things happening for you. It is worthwhile to acknowledge the presence of this star by by **placing specially-painted glass stones** with auspicious inscriptions here. The stones jiggle the Earth luck of the Southwest, strengthening the sector and bringing good fortune to the Matriarch of the household. You can do this yourself. Just get specially-empowered river stones and use your own energy to paint these stones. Best is to recite three malas of mantras before doing any painting. When finished, just blow over the stones while thinking of what series of good things you want happening for you! This is an easy cosmic ritual that is more effective than most people realize. It is like sending powerful thought energies into the Universe.

Note that there is also the *Robbery Star* in the third subsector of the Southwest, but an **Anti-Robbery Plaque** placed here should counter this troublesome star. Never forget that the luck of the Southwest affects the matriarch.

NORTHEAST
Benefitting from Heaven Luck
In the Sheep Year, this sector is strengthened by the *Star of Heavenly Seal*, which brings divine approval for your household's activities and conduct. This star brings unexpected assistance your way and those wanting strong career luck can energize this star by placing a symbol that represents the **Seal of the Emperor**.

Replicas of antique dynastic seals have become very popular as they are excellent for depicting heavenly power. Use such an Imperial Seal to activate the Northeast 3 sector. Remember that in the feng shui chart, the number 6 star placed here brings the luck of heaven, so it is auspicious to bring in symbolic representations of heaven's pure land. Pictures that depict your idea of heaven such as peaceful, colourful scenery that incorporate mountains are auspicious, especially when hung in the Northeast, the sector symbolized by mountain energy.

Unfortunately, the *Star of Heavenly Seal* is the only auspicious 24 Mountains star in the Northeast, so

2015 STARS OF THE 24 MOUNTAINS

NORTHEAST

NORTHEAST 1: Sui Po
NORTHEAST 2: Year Conflict
NORTHEAST 3: Heaven Seal

For the NORTHEAST
- Activate HEAVEN SEAL
- Appease TAI SUI with Pi Yao
- Suppress CONFLICT star with red apples

all the more reason to energize luck from heaven. In Northeast 2, there is the *Yearly Conflict Star* and in Northeast 3 there is the *Sui Po Star*, which means confronting the Tai Sui who is in the opposite direction. The best way to cope with the conflict star is to carry the Peace Amulet.. This brings harmony amongst family members. As for the clash with the Tai Sui, the placement of a **heavenly Pi Yao** should appease the Tai Sui, and keep you in his good books for the year.

HO TU COMBINATIONS 2015
BENEFITTING THE YEAR IN THE CENTER

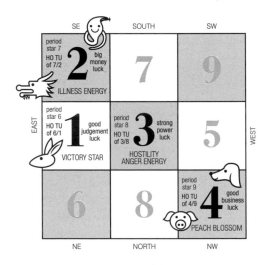

We see again the appearance of all four of the Ho Tu combinations in the Year of the Wood Sheep. These are specific combinations of the annual and period 8 numbers in four sectors of the year's grid and they benefit these sectors in homes and offices. In 2015, the sectors having the Ho Tu are different from last year. The animal signs that benefit from the Ho Tu combinations are shown in the illustration here. You can see that while the North/South axis benefits the most from the 24 Mountains, it is the Southeast/Northwest axis locations that enjoy the luck of the Ho Tu and this brings good fortune to the **Dog**.

There are three sectors in the diagonal of luck created, the Southeast, the center and the Northwest. Assessing the impact of the 24 Mountains and the Ho Tu together, we can see that 2015 brings good fortune for those with homes placed in the Southeast/Northwest axis direction i.e. facing or sitting in either of these two directions.

The animal signs that benefit directly from Ho Tu combinations include the **Dog** and the **Boar** in the Northwest, the **Dragon** and the **Snake** in the Southeast, and the **Rabbit** in the East. The complete set of auspicious Ho Tu combinations making an appearance in the year's chart, with all of them in their waxing cycles, suggests that substantial good fortune should pervade the year, especially since one of the combinations is placed in the center thereby **benefitting everyone.**

The Ho Tu is part of the comprehensive Flying Star (Xuan Kong) compass formula, probably the most effective of the time dimension formulas. It is used by many practising feng shui experts because it is easy to use and can be successfully adapted for modern homes. It is an accurate way of charting annual changes in feng shui frequencies that affect the luck of buildings (and the residents within) from year to year.

Flying Star practice requires skillful interpretation of the nine numbers placed in different compass sectors; and in picking out lucky combinations of numbers in each of the eight sectors and in the center. The numbers offer clues to the frequencies that reveal the outlook for business, health, wealth and marriage possibilities. Each number from 1 to 9 represents a particular kind of good fortune or misfortune. These vary in type and intensity from year to year.

When each of the numbers in the ANNUAL feng shui chart combines with the Period number in a Ho Tu combination i.e. as 1/6; 2/7; 3/8; and 4/9 in a specific compass sector, the combination brings **extraordinary good luck** for those who know how to activate and make the most of these combinations.

The Ho Tu combinations are an extension of the Lo Shu pattern of numbers brought on the back of a Tortoise that emerged from the River Lo. The discovery of the Lo Shu is attributed to *Fu Hsi*, the legendary emperor regarded as the founder of all things esoteric in Chinese history.

Readers familiar with feng shui will know that the Lo Shu is the magic square of nine numbered grids that is the basis of the Flying Star formula. The Lo Shu square can also be viewed as the Ho Tu square. The number 5 is in the center of the Lo Shu and the remaining numbers create four pairs of numbers that pivot around the central number of 5.

The Ho Tu combination reflects the "movement" of the numbers going round the number 5 in an anti-clockwise direction, thereby creating a left-turning swastika.

THE HO TU SQUARE &
ITS NUMBER COMBINATIONS

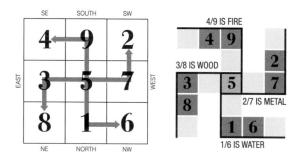

This swastika itself is a sacred symbol. It is powerful and protective. It is the symbol of Chinese Mahayana Buddhism and is often worn as an amulet. This swastika must not be confused with the Nazi swastika used by Hitler, which was right-turning with the cross being a diagonal cross.

The Ho Tu (and Buddhist) swastika comprises one vertical and one horizontal line with left-turning arms. The Nazi swastika is right-turning and it brings power but also passionate and unscrupulous ambition. The left-turning swastika brings protection and compassion.

There are four sets of numbers created by the swastika. These are **1 and 6, 2 and 7, 3 and 8 and 4 and 9** and they are collectively referred to as the Ho Tu sets of numbers. Each Ho Tu is represented by a dominant element, which when activated, causes four kinds of excellent good fortune to actualize for the sector and animal sign(s) there. In 2015 we see that:

+ In the SE, the annual star 2 combines with the Period Star 7, bringing **big money luck** to the sector and to the **Snake** and **Dragon**, both of whom have a special relationship with the Rooster.

+ In the CENTER, the annual star 3 combines with the Period Star 8, bringing **strong power** and **recognition luck**. This has the potential to affect **everyone**.

+ In the NW, the annual star 4 combines with the Period Star 9, bringing excellent **business luck** to those occupying this sector, to the **Dog** and the **Boar**.

+ In the EAST, the annual star 1 combines with the Period Star 6, bringing **excellent good judgement luck**. This is sometimes described as the wisdom combination. It brings luck to the **Rabbit** and those in pursuit of academic excellence. This combination benefits students and those still at College.

The Ho Tu has the potential to make everybody happy. If your house faces any of the three side locations blessed with the Ho Tu this year, you can benefit from the combination irrespective of your animal sign. What is important is to activate the Ho Tu by strengthening with symbols as well as with the *element* of the combination.

THE 2/7 COMBINATION *in the Southeast*

This is activated by strengthening **Metal**; by the sounds of metal emanating from the Southeast. Note that the Southeast is a Wood sector, so Metal energy must not be excessively harsh; thus just the sounds is sufficient. Do not place too many metal symbols here; perhaps a **metallic windchime** or **singing bell or bowl**. Painting the main door white or in a metallic shade is also excellent.

MONTHS ENJOYING ENHANCED HO TU
The power of 2/7 is magnified during the month of **April** and in **January 2016** when the number 2 monthly star flies to the Southeast. These are the months when some big money will arrive at your doorstep as there two Ho Tu's in the sector then.

THE 3/8 COMBINATION *in the CENTER*

The Ho Tu in the center is 3/8, which strengthens your **power and authority**. Respect for you increases if you can benefit from this Ho Tu. This combination is usually felt most in political families, although this does not mean power can be exercised easily.

In the center this year is the star of hostile misunderstandings and quarrels, so any **rise in political status** is sure to involve direct clashes with competitors. However, if you can strongly activate this Ho Tu to benefit from it directly, you are likely to win. You will also know if you should give in gracefully to fight again another day. The element to strengthen in the center, which will bring 3/8 to life, is the element of Wood. Thus placing the image of a **bejewelled tree** here is extremely beneficial. You could also place plants here but bear in mind that too much wood will strengthen the Number 3 star of hostility and cause a lot of anger to surface.

THE 4/9 COMBINATION *in the Northwest*

This combination brings **Commercial and Business success** and it is Fire element energy which will stimulate the 4/9 in the Northwest. Place **candles** here to energize the Ho Tu here but it is not necessary to be excessive. This is the sector of the Patriarch and too much Fire energy is as bad as no fire at all. The 4/9 combination brings excellent business luck which means that your monetary gains can improve when you energize this Ho Tu.

THE 1/6 COMBINATION *in the East*

This is the **Scholastic and Wisdom combination** and in 2015, it appears in the sector of the East. **Its element is Water** and having the presence of water in the East corner of your living area will simulate this Ho Tu to bring excellent luck for the ripening of wisdom realizations.

This works well for motivating young adults who may be still in College or who have just joined the workforce building themselves a career. Wisdom realizations are rare and if you have this luck, it makes you mature and grow up pretty fast, bringing beneficial common sense to your head. **Place water in a circular bowl** in the East to manifest deeper understanding of life.

HO TU MIRRORS FOR 2015
PERSONALIZED HO TU MIRRORS
To be in sync with the sectors housing this year's Ho Tu combinations

In 2015 we see a repeat of the occurrence of all four

Ho Tu combinations. Having this phenomenon two years in a row is very auspicious. It really is excellent for everyone to take the fullest advantage by activating the sectors with the Ho Tu with specially crafted personalized mirrors. These are energizing mirrors that are etched with all the necessary and relevant symbols to directly work their magic. Made of brass, these mirrors must be coloured to reflect the Element of the Ho Tu in the sector it occupies. On one side should be a polished mirror surface ringed by the *wish-granting dependent arising mantra* to empower the mirror. On the other side are all the empowering symbols needed.

The inclusion of the sun and moon to reflect the waxing energy must be present as they bring good fortune, while an image of the Dragon Horse, which originally brought the Ho Tu numbers to mankind, strengthens the sense of lineage.

3/8 Hotu Mirror

2/7 Hotu Mirror

4/9 Hotu Mirror

1/6 Hotu Mirror

These mirrors never lose their effectiveness as their power is infinite; they strengthen exponentially with the passage of time.

This is the great value of ALL good fortune brass mirrors, which is why MIRRORS must never be discarded but instead should be treasured and passed to the next generation. This really is a <u>very lucky long-term tradition</u> to start within any family. The mirrors should be kept in the family to extend all good fortune brought by the Ho Tu through the years and captured in the mirror. Let the good fortune endure!

In 2015, the Ho Tu mirrors to acquire are:

+ The **SCHOLAR-WISDOM MIRROR** to energize the 1/6 in the EAST sector which is of the WOOD element. This mirror has the image of the Rabbit, a wish-granting tree and symbols of wisdom and academic attainments. It is also excellent to include the Three Celestial Guardians to ensure protection against obstacles that block the luck of the Ho Tu. The colour of the background is green (to reflect the East sector). A water symbol or the colour blue can also be incorporated to reflect this Ho Tu combination. This mirror is an excellent gift to members of your family who are born in the year of the Rabbit or to friends belonging to this sign. This creates an invisible bond between you that will be long-lasting and happy.

This mirror can bring excellent examination luck for all school or College going children when they place it in the East corner of their study desk.

+ The **BIG MONEY MAGIC MIRROR** to activate the 2/7 in the SOUTHEAST sector which is of the WOOD element. This mirror has the two animal signs of the Snake and the Dragon, a pair of signs, which when placed together, creates magic. The luck of this Ho Tu combination is the luck of big money, which flows to those who energize this corner and empowering the spirit of the Dragon and Snake to bring you big success.

The Element of this combination is Earth, and the image of **three mountains** represents new wealth. The background colour of this mirror can be black or green. If you can also include the God of Wealth representing the Golden Deity presence in this sector, the mirror will create amazing good fortune for those who carry or display it.

+ **The POWER MIRROR** to ignite the 3/8 in the CENTER which is of the EARTH element. This is an empowering mirror, which strengthens the power of your speech and your actions. It makes people listen to you and like you. For some, this mirror will energize all the latent abilities within them. This is a strong empowerment mirror and because it is placed in the center, **this Ho Tu benefits all 12 animal signs.** It should have a red background.

This combination of Ho Tu brings excellent luck in politics. The red background has the power to silence all your critics and help you avoid the arrows of those who might want to challenge you. Energizing the sector with a mirror as described (preferably made larger) will not only help you win people over, it also suppresses all hostile energy aimed at you.

+ The **BIG PROFITS MIRROR** 4/9 in the NORTHWEST sector which is of the METAL element. This mirror should have the image of the Dog and the Boar. This Ho Tu combination will bring you steady growth in your business success. It energizes the luck of trading, bringing improved gains to all your commercial activities this year. It can also be helpful in getting you an increase in your income. The mirror should have an image of a **yang house**, preferably a mansion to signify victory over whatever YIN influences may come your way. You should also have an auspicious seal symbolizing an ocean of commercial luck from all directions. There is no need for an extra colour.

CHAPTER 4
LOVE LUCK
OF THE DOG
IN 2015

Unwilling to engage emotionally even though there are opportunities to do so...

COMPATIBILITY WITH EACH ANIMAL SIGN

COMPATIBILITY	LUCK OUTLOOK IN 2015
DOG & RAT	Not living up to expectations
DOG & OX	A passionate time for these Earth signs
DOG & TIGER	An excellent time for a fabulous pair
DOG & RABBIT	Loved up pair leans in on Rabbit's strength
DOG & DRAGON	In 2015, incompatibility gets stretched
DOG & SNAKE	Dog woos Snake, but with little success
DOG & HORSE	Allies make for an endearing pair
DOG & SHEEP	In 2015, love seems to waft sweet fragrance
DOG & MONKEY	Resilience of the Dog benefits the pairing
DOG & ROOSTER	Resentment clouds an otherwise happy relationship
DOG & DOG	Resilience of the Dog benefits the pairing
DOG & BOAR	A challenging time for this pair

LOVE LUCK OF THE DOG IN 2015
The Peach Blossom blows romantic opportunities your way but you may be unwilling to pursue them

The Dog's love life in 2015 goes through a bumpy time with one thing after another causing you to get distracted and unhappy. It is a year when few things seem to go right and aggravations confront you at every corner. And although the Dog sign enjoys the luck of the *Peach Blossom*, the 24 Mountains bring you a whole series of challenges that cause misunderstandings and hostility to arise between you and the ones you love. This can be quite an obstacle to pursuing an active social life.

The result then is a lack of inclination when it comes to getting involved in romancing-type activities despite there being opportunities to do so. In any case, the Dog suffers from a low level of spirit essence; as a result of which, you could also be feeling a lack of confidence when it comes to personal issues. Usually when one's spirit essence is weak, it tends to affect one's feelings of self-assurance. You do not want to put your ego on the line and who can blame you?

Those of you still single might also not possess the inner vitality needed to get heavily involved in the dating ritual. Do not expect to be raring to go out much this year, because the more sedentary pursuits really will suit you better. Those ensconced comfortably in an existing relationship e.g. those already married or living with someone – are likely to be placing attention on other aspects of your life.

The Dog in 2015 is not all that interested in any kind of chase that involves an investment of feelings. You prefer to get yourself involved in self-improvement type activities, or better yet, ally yourself or lend your time and name to supporting some worthwhile course.

There is insufficient motivation for the Dog to get excited about matters of the heart, and if anything, you would probably just go with the flow. In 2015, you resist many attempts to engage emotionally.

Your main focus in 2015 will be on social and educational work rather than on spending time participating in romantic pursuits; this in spite of the influence of feng shui winds that bring the number 4 *Star of Romance*. The **45 year old Metal Dog** is motivated by activities that hold out the promise of financial gains and an enhancement of status. For instance, the pursuit of business activities is something that will make the Dog more enthusiastic.

The **33 year old Water Dog** is not as motivated by work as its older counterpart, but for you, it will be educational pursuits that get you excited. Thus you are likely to consider going back to University or getting yourself involved in some research program. For those of you still single, romance is likely to find its way to you quite seamlessly then through your pursuit of new directions of learning.

> The Dog in 2015 is unlikely to get swept up in any sort of whirlwind romance, although you can see yourself getting married to someone already going out with you in a committed relationship.

This is the year when the Dog sign enjoys the *Star of the Peach Blossom* and planning for a *hei see*, a happiness event, is something that benefits you and brings you luck. It is a seamless blending with the feng shui winds of the year. This would fit well into the energy flow of the **33 year old Water Dog.** Should you feel an inner resistance to getting married, it is a good idea to convince yourself to do so.

Both the male as well as female Dog however will not be strongly inclined towards marriage or starting any hot romance this year. You are simply feeling anti-social and this is due to the influence of the *Yearly Killing Star*, on which your sign sits. You are also affected by the *Star of the Yin House* and the *Three Killings*, the two stars which flank your home location of Northwest 1.

These are negative stars, which have a depressing effect on the sign of the Dog this year. Indeed, it is actually good for you to be more sociable and to enjoy the company of others rather than allow yin energies to get you down and make you reluctant to socialize.

This is not to say you cannot be persuaded by good friends. The Dog person will usually fall in with the plans of those near and dear. As long as whatever is required does not distract you from your other commitments, you are always happy to oblige when others invite you out.

For the Dog who is already in a relationship, the year is likely to be uneventful in terms of your love luck. Those in a live-in relationship might well toy with the idea of marriage or even starting a family, and if you do so, it is likely to be auspicious in the long term. In fact, getting married can be the catalyst to good fortune ripening for the Dog. And as far as marriage is concerned, this is a promising year for the Dog as your sign enjoys the *Peach Blossom Star*.

For the already married **45 year old Metal Dog**, your marriage situation is likely to benefit from excellent wealth-enhancing luck, so financially, this is an exciting year for you. But you might have some health problems this year that might cause strains to the relationship.

For the **57 year old Earth Dog,** this could turn out to be a strenuous year when there will be strains on both your health and wealth luck. From this perspective, the year is likely to be quite challenging indeed, and your marriage could be affected as a result. However, the Dog sign is usually very good at keeping whatever is stressing them out to themselves rather than sharing it with their spouse. The generous nature of this sign includes bearing whatever burdens that come their way very much by itself.

For the Dog who might be contemplating marriage this year, it is beneficial to investigate your astrological compatibility using your respective animal signs. Here are eight things you might wish to check out to enhance the chances of marriage working out happily for you.

ONE *Same Kua Group*
Check if you and your potential partner belong to

the same Kua group either **East** or **West**. You do not need to belong to the same group to be compatible but when you are of the same group it is easier to create good feng shui that brings harmony and happiness into marriage relationships.

TWO *Sum-of-Ten*

Check if the two of you enjoy any of the auspicious Kua **sum-of-ten combinations** when your two Kua numbers combine. An example is when you are Kua 3 and your potential partner is Kua 7, then the two of you represent a beautiful, complete whole. In this case then, whether you belong to the same or different groups, your union is auspicious for both. Note that 3 and 7 belong to the East and West groups respectively, so you will need to work hard at being mutually supportive for the coming future. It is beneficial to note that the combination of similar numbers is not as auspicious as the sum-of-ten combinations.

THREE *Ho Tu Combinations*

Check if the two of you have Kua numbers that make up one of the four lucky **Ho Tu combinations** of 1/6, 2/7, 3/8 and 4/9. When two people within a partnership or marriage have a Ho Tu relationship created by their Kua numbers, the outcome of their life together tends to be auspicious.

Those with **1 and 6** Kuas tend to be very clever people who excel professionally in the arts and sciences; you can create a wonderful life together because you have intellectual compatibility.

Those with a **2 and 7** Kua number combination will get rich as a couple, as your life together can bring out big money luck for you both.

Those with **3 and 8** Kuas enjoy admirable social status and influence; you have a future together as leaders or as style setters. This combination indicates a life of power and authority.

When your Kua numbers are **4 and 9** together, you enjoy excellent business luck as a partnership; if the two of you get into a JV enterprise, you will be sure to succeed and make good profits.

FOUR Secret Friends

Check if the two of you are astrological **Secret Friends** – here we are referring to a pairing of the **Dog** with the **Rabbit**; this is a very exciting pairing as there will be wonderful support for each other. Being each other's secret friend means it is harder for outside third parties to drive a wedge between the two of you. There is hence a higher probability of fidelity and faithfulness. The Dog is excellent for the Rabbit, and vice versa.

FIVE *Astrological Allies*

Check if you and your potential partner are **Astrological Allies**. Being each other's ally introduces the all-important attributes of loyalty and sensitivity. You are sure to like each other in addition to the loving, so there is wonderful potential for happiness. The **Dog** has two allies, the **Tiger** and the **Horse**. The three of you make up the adventurous and rebellious trinity of the Zodiac. When you live with either the Horse or the Tiger, you are likely to make all sorts of plans to venture into the unknown or take up some popular new cause. This is in your nature – supporting the underdog or adopting a cause that make you feel you are giving back to the world.

SIX *Soulmate Pairing*

Check if the two of can create a **Soulmate Pairing** that creates something special together. For the **Dog**, note that you have a very special relationship with those from the sign of the **Boar,** as the two of you form the *House of Domesticity* together. This suggests that if the Dog and Boar get together and marry, you can have an idealistic family life full of love, laughter and children, amidst an atmosphere of domestic bliss.

The two of you enjoy a powerful relationship with one another, and you can build a fulfilling life together, taking pleasure in both the small and the big life events.

SEVEN *Paht Chee Compatibility*

Check if you have each other's Chinese Zodiac Signs in your **Paht Chee**. If your animal sign is present in your partner's Paht Chee chart as the MONTH pillar, it means that the relationship is auspicious and you will hold the power in the relationship. If your animal sign is in his DAY pillar, you are evenly matched and neither will be dominant. If your sign is in his HOUR pillar however, it means you are compatible and you are happy to be in the subordinate role in the relationship.

EIGHT *Arrows of Antagonism*

Finally, check if you are in a naturally hostile situation with each other in terms of **Astrological Non-Compatibility**. You should try not to hook up with your astrological foe the Dragon. This is the animal sign located directly opposite you in the astrology compass. The long term outcome is rarely happy or good. The probability of the two of you separating can then be quite high. The **Dog** and **Dragon** are better off not marrying or living together as partners. Even when there is love flowing back and forth during the initial stages, you are unlikely to be close over the long term. Note however that astrological opposites can co-exist quite harmoniously as friends or siblings.

****

In 2015, the already married Dog is unlikely to bring any new excitement to their marriage. Yours is a comfortable staid life this year, and you are better off being low profile than having too busy a social life. If you have been together for many years, accept that you need your own space this year.

In any case, there could also be sad occasions that get you down, so it is better to let the sad times lift your levels of intimacy with each other, instead of letting them cause silent resentment to rise up between you. Look on the trials and tribulations of this year as life obstacles to be faced. Have faith in each other.

The Dog's Life Force is good, so there is vitality in the relationship, but success indications in your element chart are weak due to your very low level of *lung ta* energy. Your spirit essence is also weak. What this means is that the Dog experiences challenges and difficulties that can cause misunderstandings. Those around you need to be understanding.

For the single Dog, 2015 may be a good time get married. This creates the energy to help you snap you out of your yin energy tendencies. A *hei see*, or happiness occasion, gives a boost of vitality to your life. And if you have only just met someone and your relationship progresses very quickly, it is because of the *Peach Blossom Star* this year is speeding up marriage luck for you. Those already in a committed relationship will need to depend on your partner to bring you good luck.

THE MALE DOG

In 2015, the Dog gentleman needs to actively cultivate a state of repose and relaxation; this should help you shrug off the burdens of the year and help you feel light and hang loose. Your attitude this year can be quite glum, but it is a year that can bring you a new and unexpected love interest. This is sure to give your love life a lift, and even though you may deny it to yourself, your inner resilience will bounce back and your natural instincts will surface.

This is when the normally happy amiable Dog personality surfaces. This is the affectionate, friendly and faithful side of the Dog persona. Even your outward appearance will improve as you pull yourself together. Make an effort to let go of the dour expression and reject cynicism completely.

In 2015 the Dog guy is best when surrounded by loving energy. Develop positive expectations and make yourself feel optimistic about life and about your future. You have so many attributes and this makes you a popular guy to have around.

> The Dog gentleman should not lack confidence or courage. This is an excellent year for you to rediscover your life's purpose. Allow yourself to be inspired by new goals and let yourself be distracted by love, sex and the promise of a new relationship.

All these developments are sure to bring you out of your lethargy. Once you get your chi energy moving, you will feel a great deal better. Dog guys tend to be be fastidious and industrious. You work well and rise to great heights when motivated; the problem is that the Dog sign is rarely ambitious in a conventional sense. Success is important to you, but never at any cost! You are not looking for the pot of gold at the end of the rainbow. Dog men are easily contented and as soon as the Dog guy reaches a plateau in his career, he is quite happy to spend his days researching, analyzing and criticizing the ills of mankind. Hence Dogs rarely like being hot shot corporate or busy business people.

What is important to him? Justice! The environment! Human rights! Global warming! The rainforests of the world, the lofty and noble causes of today's world. The Dog sign will speak out loudly and fearlessly, but he is practical and down-to-earth. The Dog will not stick his neck out, nor endanger himself or his family by being a rebel.

The Dog is not martyr material. But he is loyal and possesses great charm. The Dog makes a devoted friend and an affectionate companion. At a personal level, he is the giver. In his personal relationships, he goes for the overkill and could quite easily overwhelm you with his acts of benevolence.

THE FEMALE DOG

The Dog lady is also a very loyal friend; a great wife, an excellent mother and a kindly supporting sister. These traits are always evident no matter what kind of year it is. In 2015 however, the Dog woman could seem a little distracted as she needs to cope with a variety of setbacks and disappointments. Despite the crosses she has to bear this year, the Dog lady continues to be generous with her time and effort expended on other people's behalf. Despite friendly advice to be less committed, the Dog woman's world is wrapped around feel-good causes. To her, life is about helping others; the more successful and well off she is, the more intense she is about getting involved in charitable pursuits.

Dog ladies who work also bring intensity to their working life, and because they are careful and rather plodding in their approach to work, they earn the respect of peers and subordinates alike, but their bosses and supervisors usually tend to take advantage of their good nature.

Despite all the smiles however the Dog lady tends towards pessimism, as if they cannot believe their good luck when things go well for them, and in their life. The Dog lady generally has a load of misgivings, anticipating imaginary problems and exhibiting a natural caution that can be extremely tiresome to those working with her. In the end however, she delivers on her promises, and all the worry that precedes victory or success is instantly forgotten. In 2015 she may not be so lucky, as it is a year devoid of much good news; but she nevertherless perseveres and makes a most reliable friend.

In 2015, the Dog lady is in a weaker state emotionally and is unlikely to be a good source of tender loving care. In matters of love and romance, it is easy to take advantage of her easy, trusting nature. She is aware of this, but in 2015, love is on her side.

Emotionally, the Dog woman develops maturity late in life. Many Dog women however find it hard to shake off their attitude of pessimism and those have this tendency end up as spinsters! Unless she can find someone to strengthen her emotional make up, those still alone late in life find it hard to connect with a potential spouse. Having said this, 2015 is a good year to keep your eyes open. This year, love is on your side.

ACTIVATING MARRIAGE LUCK

Those of you wishing to improve your chances of finding someone special or wanting to magnify your marriage luck can use the powerful method of activating your *Peach Blossom Marriage Luck*. For the Dog, your **Peach Blossom Animal** is the **Rabbit** the cardinal animal sign of the East, so activating the East corner of your bedroom, or of your most frequently-used room with a nice-looking Rabbit image should open greater opportunities to you. Get a Rabbit that is robust and handsome, because the better-looking the Rabbit is, the better will be the potential husband or wife that you can attract.

> Do not to get a cheap-looking Rabbit image from shops that look rundown or shifty. Buy your feng shui Peach Blossom Enhancer from a shop or from someone who makes you feel good about yourself! Energy associated with the Peach Blossom animal must be vigorous, positive and classy.

The Dog can activate for marriage luck by placing their Peach Blossom animal the Rabbit in the East of their bedroom.

PEACH BLOSSOM SYMBOLS FOR THE 12 ANIMAL SIGNS

🐇 **RABBIT**	Horse, Tiger, Dog			East
🐴 **HORSE**	Rooster, Snake, Ox			South
🐓 **ROOSTER**	Dragon, Monkey, Rat			West
🐀 **RAT**	Rabbit, Sheep, Boar			North

Your PEACH BLOSSOM animal, the Rabbit placed in the East activates romance luck in 2015

Marriage and romance manifests differently for each of the five kinds of Dog. Activating *Peach Blossom Luck* does help in opening doorways to love, but it is really beneficial to investigate how the Dog interacts with each of the twelve signs of the Zodiac this year.

The indications given here are analysed from the year's charts and thus point to likely scenarios of luck for two signs coming together. For compatibility over the long term, you should always be guided by the checklist given earlier in this chapter.

DOG/RAT

In 2015, not living up to expectations

This does not turn out to be such a great match in 2015 because the reality of romance between the Dog and the Rat will not pan out as wonderful as both might at first hope for. The year is unlikely to be conducive to the two of you getting into a romantic relationship, despite elements of romance surrounding the Dog. Unfortunately, neither of you are feeling very much in the mood for heavy romance this year!

> The match of Dog and Rat is astrologically unexciting, despite some good vibes making an intermittent appearance in 2015, although hardly frequently enough to let the two of you make a go of things. Both of you are simply not that good for each other, mainly because you tend to bring out the worst in each other. When this happens, many things will get said that become difficult to swallow back when tempers cool.

In the heat of disagreement, the two of you could tend to be more hurtful than you each mean to be, but that is the way it will come out. There will be some sort of antagonism that rises to the surface. In 2015, there are good moments that can arise because the Rat is enjoying an auspicious year. Unfortunately, the Rat is insecure this year, and without knowing why, the Rat acts resentful of criticism. The two signs are so obviously incompatible that resentment erupts all the time. As such, whatever romance that may have arisen will simply fly out the window.

> The Dog can feel passionate about the Rat in 2015, so the Dog might well start a romance; unfortunately, with the Rat, feelings do not go deep enough.

The Dog is usually loyal within a marriage, but in this match, the Dog is likely to be put off by what he/she perceives as the Rat's insensitive behaviour. It does not take long for these perceptions to take root in the Dog's mind. Meanwhile, the Rat finds that the Dog's initial warm-hearted nature does not last, and thus starts to mistrust and question the Dog's motives. This non-communication causes a great deal of barking, and instead of getting better over the years, this match gets a whole lot worse. The Rat's insecure nature gets in the way of there being any genuine communication, and the Dog simply gives up trying to make things work and will instead look elsewhere for love.

This match can end up sad and loveless, as each of the signs will retreat into his/her own shell. The chill between you is unlikely to thaw over time.

DOG/OX

In 2015, a passionate time for these Earth signs

The Dog and Ox enjoy the special *sum-of-ten* combination, so should you come together as a couple this year, it will benefit you both. The Ox's number is 6 and it combines with the Dog's number 4 to create the sum-of-ten, bringing a wholeness that can draw the two of you very close and bring you much happiness as well. It causes the attraction between the two of you to be full of mutual trust and respect.

The Dog is likely to be feeling more romantic in 2015 than the Ox, but happily, the Ox is more than willing to move with the flow.

The Dog/Ox pairing is one of mutual love and admiration. Although the Dog likes to think it is in command, it will be the Ox who wields greater influence in the relationship. The Ox however is skillful and will not let the Dog feel manipulated.

The Ox takes everything the Dog says with a gravity that is admirable, but in the end, the Ox has the knack of getting its way without being confrontational. In 2015, the Dog gains from riding on the good fortune coattails of the Ox, who benefits from *Big Auspicious* luck. The Ox also has other exciting new opportunities brought by the heaven luck it enjoys this year. As a pair, your energies weave together to bring you sweet success. Together you can build something that has the potential to become quite big.

> While the Ox is the industrious and hard-working half of the pair, the Dog lends an air of ease and effortlessness to your pursuits together. As a couple, you have the ability to soar up high, while keeping your feet planted firmly on the ground. Both the Ox and Dog are faithful and loyal by nature, so your union is unlikely to be dogged by problems of infidelity.

You bring out a sense of security in each other, which bodes well for a long future. Of the two, there will be more temptations for the Dog when it comes to external dalliances, but if the Ox does not give the Dog a reason to stray, it won't. It nevertheless does not do any harm for you both to wear the **anti-infidelity amulet**, not so much to stop you from being naughty, but to prevent outside parties from coming in to spoil things for you.

A wonderful pairing indeed, one you should work to protect at all costs.

DOG/TIGER

In 2015, an excellent time for a fabulous pair

For these astrological allies, the year 2015 will turn out to be quite a fabulous time. Your energies mesh beautifully and there is a magical completion to this pairing this year. Things will turn out extremely well for you both. There is growth and success, and there is also a lot of love and caring.

> This is also a fabulously well-matched pair. Here we are talking about a totally darling Dog and an equally engaging Tiger! Cannot imagine Cat and Dog loving up to one another? Actually it should not be difficult, as there is truly good compatibility between the two of you.

You will find yourselves enjoying the year's good fortune vibes. The Tiger is headed for success, while the Dog is feeling especially romantic this year. Your natural affinity will enhance your happiness and help you sail through what will be a fabulous year for you. The Dog understands the Tiger's impetuous nature completely, and is prepared to stay indulgent. The Tiger meanwhile comprehends the Dog's altruistic attitude, the need to do good for others, even to the point of being a busy body or going out of the way to help a friend in need. So the Tiger does not resent being controlled or nagged at. Indeed, there is a great deal of mutual respect in this relationship and the ferocious Tiger becomes a pussycat with the Dog! It is an adorable match that can surely last a long time.

The Dog's natural element is Earth, while the Tiger's natural element is Wood. In the cycle of element relationships, Wood destroys Earth. One party is therefore clearly dominant of the other, and in this case, it is the Tiger that dominates and is in control. But here the Dog does not mind. Their natural affinity softens the Tiger's touch and the Dog is content to let the Tiger be in charge!

FENG SHUI TIP: For the Dog already with a Tiger, what should make things even better is to get an *image of the Boar* (the Tiger's secret friend) and place in the Northwest sector of the bedroom you share together.

DOG/RABBIT

In 2015, loved up pair leans in on Rabbit's strength

The Dog and Rabbit are two signs that have the potential to resonate with a great loving energy this year. In 2015, this pair of secret friends is extremely blessed as you enjoy the kind of luck that leads to a happy and fruitful marriage. You have the potential to create a wonderful family together. Those of you currently dating and thinking of settling down will meet few obstacles standing in your way. You are compatible, reasonable, extremely nice to one another and temperamentally well-suited.

The Dog & Rabbit have a real chance of finding happiness together, especially in 2015, which brings romantic luck vibrations to the Dog. But it is the Rabbit who brings the good fortune vibrations that benefit you both.

You both enjoy *Peach Blossom* romanticism. The year's charts indicate that feng shui winds and astrological indications are also favourable. This match brings two solid and stable individuals together, and in 2015, we also see great sparks of passion radiating from this couple. There is plenty to smile about, so joyous laughter is part of your destiny this year. The two of you are likely to generate a great deal of happiness energy, so nothing tedious or boring about this pair.

> You are a couple who sticks together through thick and thin. Indeed, if any pairing can overcome adversity, this pair can. You are well-matched and loving towards each other in good times as well as bad. In 2015, you will see some great happiness moments, which you should embrace with vitality and gusto.

You will never be fairweather friends and indeed you inspire great depths of feelings in one another, so your life together is sure to be very happy. It will be a relationship characterized by supportive energy and cooperative support. It is a secure relationship, where problems get dealt with calmly, and where differences never develop into big disagreements.

The Dog and Rabbit are loyal by nature, so any chance of either doing anything to upset the other is quite remote. The Rabbit's element of Wood controls the Dog's element of Earth. It will be the Rabbit who sets the tone and pace of this relationship, but the yin-yang configuration of this pair brings wonderful balance to the union and it will make sense for the Dog to lean in on the Rabbit for inner and outer strength.

DOG/DRAGON

♥

In 2015, incompatibility gets stretched

The Dog and Dragon are evenly matched in 2015, but
it will be the Dragon who has the slightly upper hand.
It is a year when the natural incompatibility between
the two of you gets stretched, and it is unlikely you
will even find one another attractive. Both the Dog
and Dragon are Earth signs and both are yang.
This preponderance of Earth and *yang* energy will
accentuate tempers, so it may be best for you to look
elsewhere for love.

> The hostility between you is sure to
> bring out all your naturally aggressive
> tendencies, and for the Dog, you might
> even be goaded into snarling your way
> out of the relationship in 2015.

The Dog sign simply does not have the patience or the
strength to cope with a weary, sick Dragon. There is
neither love nor goodwill feelings, and when it comes
to the crunch, neither of you can pretend to be nice or
caring. With the year's energies weakening these two
signs, it is really better to stay apart.

In addition to the natural antipathy between you, 2015
sees the Dog's energy at a physically vulnerable level;

the Dragon too is likely to be short tempered and neither sign has the patience to be tolerant. As a result, neither can maintain even a simple conversation with the other without either one of you getting irritated. In short, you are likely to get aggravated with one another quite a lot this year. And you would do better not to point fingers at each other. The fault lies in the stars!

It is a good idea to look elsewhere if you are looking for long term happiness; those already in a permanent relationship can place either one's astrological "**secret friend**" to create greater harmony.

In the Zodiac, your signs are placed directly in the path of each other's arrow of antagonism, hence potential for discord is high. And with the year's energies being less than conducive to both the Dragon and the Dog, it will be a hard ride staying together as a couple.

The Dog is disdainful of the Dragon's ideas and opinions; and the Dragon finds the Dog unsupportive and a wet blanket! The match is a serious example of clashing personalities. Not only is there little communication between you, there is much exhaling in exasperation on the part of the Dragon, and a great deal of barking from the Dog!

DOG/SNAKE

Dog woos Snake, but with little success in 2015

The Dog sign woos the Snake with love and romance, but has little success, as the Snake sign will be indifferent to overtures that come on too strong. This is a year when the Dog will do its level best to be sweetness and roses; there are definitely good feelings that lead to good affinity during the early months of the year. But this relationship will face obstacles and Snake is not necessarily in the mood for love.

The year does not favour the Dog too much, and in this pairing, the Snake finds the Dog's advances tiresome. In any case, the Dog sign simply cannot identify with the Snake's intense but secretive nature, which also hides lofty ambitions.

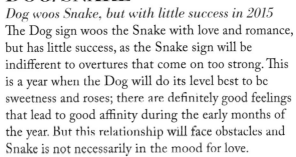

The two signs are so different in thinking and outlook because while the Dog is talkative, tending to analyze things to death, the Snake is exactly the opposite, preferring to keep things locked up in the heart.

The Dog is a frank and straightforward person, and this direct and naively forthright nature makes it hard for him/her to cope with the subtle, conniving ways of the Snake. Besides, the Dog is rarely as passionately ambitious as the Snake personality. Loyal, yes, and idealistic as well, but the Snake is practical and all knowing. The Snake can see what the Dog cannot, so usually, people of the Dog sign can rarely understand the Snake and vice versa.

This is definitely not a meeting of the minds here, as there is also not much appreciation of each other's intellect. In many instances, the Dog is not clever enough to excite and thrill the Snake for long; indeed, the Snake can deceive the Dog and even play with his/her emotions.

In 2015 this pair is better off with others. This is not a relationship borne of great mutual respect, so in fairness to both signs, they are better off finding happiness with someone else.

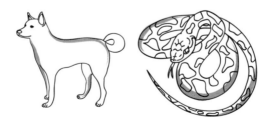

DOG/HORSE

Allies make for an endearing pair in 2015

The Dog and Horse are astrological allies and a pairing between these two signs make a very endearing couple in 2015. The two of you find love with each other quite effortlessly, influenced by the Dog's star of *Peach Blossom,* and with you being allies, you two are very simpatico. You possess the same values and your aspirations find fertile ground with each other. There is room for a great deal of real conversation to flow, so despite it being a rough year for the Horse, having a true friend like the Dog makes up for many things.

In 2015, the Horse finds calm and restful loving energy from the Dog, who strengthens the Horse's sense of self worth. The two of you can also take the year off and focus on each other instead of participating in the rat race and chasing material success, because that route will only bring frustration.

The Year of the Sheep is when love and romance holds out more promise of happiness for this pair than pursuing career promotion and business gains. And since you are both people who love adventure and travel, it is not a bad idea to consider taking an extended holiday exploring some part of the world that holds out the promise of adventure for you.

Those setting up house will find that yours is a peaceful home, with a noticeable absence of anger and temper tantrums. This is because you are prepared to give in to each other most of the time. There is cooperation and communication between you, and even when the Horse occasionally gets restive, it does not affect the relationship. This is because the Dog is patient with the Horse.

Professionally, the Horse is more courageous and perhaps more aggressive than the Dog, but 2015 is not a year to take risks at work or in business; better to keep a low profile and lean on each other instead. It really is for the better that you focus on being devoted to each other. The good thing is neither of you are the possessive or interfering type, and as a result, you do give each other space. This makes for a happy long-term relationship.

The Dog's natural element is Earth while the Horse's natural element is Fire. In the cycle of element relationships, Fire produces Earth. One party is therefore clearly supportive of the other, and in this case, it is the Horse that supports and provides for the Dog. Your natural affinity to each other makes the headstrong Horse more than happy to do so, and the Dog will appreciate the Horse's loving generosity!

DOG/SHEEP

In 2015 love seems to waft sweet fragrance

What a romantic year this could turn out to be for the Sheep who meets and falls for someone belonging to the sign of the Dog. This is the Sheep's year and its chi is strong indeed, reflecting its good life force. The Sheep walks around with stars in its eyes, and on meeting the handsome Dog sign, can fall in love, although the attraction is not deep and this actually becomes something of a saccharin relationship.

In this match, the Dog's instincts tend to be protective of the Sheep because of the seeming vulnerability of the Sheep sign. The Dog is enamoured of the Sheep, so on the surface at least, this is a pairing that generates happiness and meaningful satisfaction, especially for the Dog. The Sheep however loves being in love, and is likely to enjoy every single moment of a love relationship with the Dog.

The Sheep of course is far from helpless, and for sure is also not vulnerable in any way. If anything, it is the Sheep who might take advantage of the Dog's kind nature; but happily, it is possible that the match can lead to marriage. Indeed, this is a pair that can be so enamoured of one another they emit the sweet fragrance of romance and bring each other great happiness. Whatever differences there are between the two will be cleverly suppressed, with each taking turns to do so. In the flush of romantic love, the year carries them along. If there is a baby in the relationship, the pairing will work despite there being hidden tensions, and this is because the Dog is instinctively a family person, and it is unlikely that he/she will abandon the Sheep for greener pastures.

Here, note that both Dog & Sheep have a strongly developed sense of duty. Marriage founded on this kind of positive principles have a great chance of succeeding.

The Sheep's natural element is Earth. The Dog's element is also Earth. This preponderance of Earth imbues the relationship with pragmatism. Both parties put in good effort to make the match work, so the likelihood of happiness together is good.

DOG/MONKEY

Resilience of the Dog benefits the pairing in 2015

The chi energy of the year is friendly to a pairing between Monkey and Dog, and this is because the two of you play host to Flying Star numbers that combine to form the auspicious *Ho Tu* combination of 9/4, which brings great recognition luck and a rise in status. The combination also brings a deluge of romantic energy which both enjoy hugely.

> In actual fact, the two of you have very different attitudes, but this is a pairing that is quite unbalanced. Both sides acknowledge it and both sides accept it. Here the Monkey holds the upper hand and the Dog is happy to fall in with whatever the Monkey wants or wishes.

But for many Monkey/Dog matches, strong initial attraction can dissipate, with the danger that you could end up separating. But neither sign will be heartbroken for long. Those who continue on with each other and go on to make a life together can find that living together can be quite trying. There can be irksome disappointments because neither of you can live up to the other's expectations. And yet this is a pairing that bring magical energies into your lives, so in spite of personal disappointments with each other, the two of you can build a madly successful life together, bringing up wonderful children and creating a happy household.

All this is achieved against a background of great personal unhappiness due mainly to Monkey's habit of taking the Dog for granted. The Dog simply cannot tolerate Monkey's nonchalant dishonesty. Love can then turn into resentment and any respect that originally defined the relationship can fly out the window. But in 2015, the chi energy is so favourable to this couple that big problems are made small and small problems are ignored!

Herein lies the strength of this relationship, and it is mainly due to the tenacity of the Dog. In 2015, the Monkey receives a sudden epiphany and has a realization of the true worth of this pairing, not least the depth of the Dog's loyalty. The Monkey might lose patience with the Dog's righteous attitudes, but with the energies of the year favouring this couple, there is no resentment in this relationship. The yang Monkey's element is Metal. The Dog, also Yang, has Earth as its element. In the cycle, Earth produces Metal. It is the Dog who sustains and works at this relationship. The Monkey could lack the staying power. If it does work, credit must go to the resilience of the Dog sign.

DOG/ROOSTER

In 2015, resentment clouds an otherwise happy relationship

The Dog and Rooster might have to endure a difficult year when you both need to adjust to one another's moods. In 2015, your luck attributes are so unequal that hidden resentment can surface to cast shadows on your relationship. Despite there being genuine attraction and admiration between you, unfortunately, neither of you are immune to the harsh reality of one being luckier than the other.

> The respect you have for each other is real, as is the warm feeling of love that makes you a couple. Unfortunately for some reason, you cannot bring yourself to share your deepest emotions with one another even though you are generally demonstrative with hugs and warm embraces.

When the Dog and Rooster first get together, you can talk quite a bit with each other, but your communication tends to be superficial rather than deep. The two of you skirt around issues that reveal your hidden feelings; although you both give voice to lofty ideals, you do not really listen to each other. The moral high ground is the Dog's favourite topic of conversation. He/she takes pride in the nobler instincts of Man. Virtues like honour, integrity and loyalty are important to the Dog, but in expounding on these virtues, the Dog ignores the viewpoint and sensitivity of the Rooster. As a result, there is a great deal of switching off on the part of the Rooster, except that in 2015, hidden resentments will surface.

The Dog went through a time of bad luck, but this year, things have eased and good things come to the Dog compared with the Rooster, who is not so lucky this year; so the balance of the relationship is not conducive to feelings of warmth. Nevertheless, the Dog is unlikely to abandon the Rooster.

> In 2015, the Dog has an enormous capacity for love. So despite dark moods rising on the part of the Rooster, the Dog partner in the relationship will hang on.

Fortunately, the Rooster sign is unlikely to walk away from a good relationship. And because the Rooster is strong and confident in 2015, it is unlikely to act foolishly or impulsively. More likely, its admiration for the Dog's sterling qualities will help it ride through the relationship. The energy of the year encourages both to overlook setbacks. The year thus ends on a happy note for the both of you.

DOG/DOG

Resilience of the Dog benefits the pairing in 2015
This could work out to be a good year for two Dogs to find love with each other. It is an unlikely pairing of course, as there will always be a constant struggle for superiority and dominance, but in 2015, experiencing sad moments together can cause the two of you to develop a closeness that becomes something more.

The energy around the Dog sign in 2015 is loving and potentially happy, due to the influence of the *Peach Blossom Star,* but it is also a year when the Dog sits on the *Star of Yearly Killings* with the *Star of Yin House* next to you. This often indicates some kind of loss in the family or of someone very close. For the two of you then it could be quite a traumatic year. But 2015 is also a year when you may be thrown together, so it might become the most natural thing for you to start a relationship.

> But when two Dog signs get together, life can become a series of temper tantrums. You might find yourselves squabbling over the silliest things amidst an atmosphere of fatigue and frustration. So it is important to not rush into a relationship despite you being pushed together.

Compatibility is an important issue and the two of you together can become a dark union. You might not be able to bring happiness to each other despite the Dog personality being quite amiable. Nevertheless, the Dog can be moody too, and discerning when it comes to demonstrating loyalty.

One simply cannot take the Dog's positive attributes and qualities for granted, especially as Dogs tend to reserve their most aggressive tendencies towards their own signs.

The danger of 2015 is that the two might tie the knot in haste and when the chi energy turns negative, you may want to split. Dog signs easily develop scenarios when you become really quite confrontational with one another, and that is when loving feelings fly out the window.

Hostility then makes it hard to be rational, and common sense is unlikely to prevail. If the two of you get together, you need to work at cooling your aggressive tendencies. Learn to appreciate each other; otherwise it may be better not to get hitched to each other in the first place. In any case, the year does not make it easy for a union of two Dog people.

DOG/BOAR

In 2015 a challenging time for this pair

The personal luck element of the Dog and Boar are really not all that conducive to the two of you getting together. The energy of the year is weak for both of you, and this makes this an unlikely year to develop a relationship that can make it into the long-term. This is because both your astrological element charts indicate an overall weakness of spirit essence and *lung ta*, as a result of which there will be hidden obstacles you are both unwilling or unable to deal with.

Ordinarily, the two of you would be quite loved up as you share a compass location together and are each other's soulmates, and this year, the Northwest is visited by the *Peach Blossom Star*. But your astrological influences make this a challenging time for you both. Hence it might not be a good idea to get involved or start a new relationship in 2015.

Yet the Dog and Boar share one wonderful thing in common, and that is your very amiable and accommodating natures. You can be so sweet and nice and caring with each other. This is why there is a real possibility for the two of you to come together in a love match should you connect.

Those of you who do can expect there to be plenty of warmth and intimacy. It will be spontaneous, and a deep and abiding affection can arise quite quickly between you. Loyalty and support of each other comes naturally to you, so you are likely to stay true to one another.

As long as you both understand that 2015 is not exactly the best time for either of you to get involved in a love relationship, perhaps then your expectations will not be so high, and you can then both take fullest advantage of the *Peach Blossom energies* and develop a relationship that is happy and long-lasting.

Both the Dog and Boar have a healthy sexual appetite for each other, so yours becomes a happy and fulfilled pairing. If anything can create setbacks for the two of you, it is likely to be Boar's tendency to take advantage of the Dog's good nature. But this is part of your thing, so the yang Dog and yin Boar should be left to sort out your relationship yourselves; and you always do.

The Dog's natural element is Earth. That of the Boar is Water. In the cycle of element relationships, Earth destroys Water, which indicates it is likely the Dog who will be the dominant one in full control in this union.

CHAPTER 5
ANALYSING YOUR LUCK EACH MONTH
Redefining happiness and finding contentment in other areas of life...

For the Dog, 2015 is unlikely to be a year for madly chasing success in the work or business arena. You find much more happiness if you balance out your life, giving as much if not more focus to your family and your loved ones. Spend time cultivating your friendships and your relationships. Those of you ready to settle down should think seriously of marriage – you benefit from the Peach Blossom energies favouring your sign this year, and thinking ahead to building your family will ultimately bring you greater satisfaction and contentment than going after that promotion or searching in vain for the big break that seems a long time coming. When you allow your happiness to materialize for you in other ways, success takes on a whole new meaning, and 2015 becomes a year to remember, for all the right reasons.

FIRST MONTH
FEBRUARY 4TH - MARCH 5TH 2015

SUM-OF-TEN INDICATES A VERY AUSPICIOUS START TO THE YEAR

The Year of the Sheep starts off well for the Dog, with the *Heaven Star* bringing new opportunities your way. The number 6 star also combines with the annual number 4 star in your chart to bring you completion luck. This indicates you can get things finished. Projects and initiatives you have put time and effort into come to a successful close, but what this also means is that it may be time to look forward and onward into the future. Many of you will meet up with choices to make that will affect major aspects of your life for the coming year. But you can take comfort in the fact that you have an unseen hand helping you. Your instincts prove helpful and you can trust your inner guide to lead you down the right path. You also benefit from *Mentor Luck*, so take the counsel of those in positions to help you seriously. Accept assistance offered to you graciously, and allow the month to work its magic.

WORK & CAREER - *Working Smart*

To realize your full potential this month, you'll need the support of your boss. Putting in extra effort in developing a close relationship with your superiors will pay off more than putting in extra time slogging it. While you may be talented at working hard, you need to think outside the box and work smart as well. This is a time when it is not just the ability to get the job done that will earn you the accolades needed to move up the career ladder. It is also about how much you are liked, and how well you fit into the scheme of things in the long run. Set yourself definite objectives to meet to help you direct your energies in a constructive manner. Your fortunes are good and there are real prospects for promotion if you plays your cards right.

BUSINESS - *Proper Planning*

Business luck is promising. Use this auspicious period to bid for new projects and to secure new contracts. Your luck is riding high, so make full use of this time to think of ways you can grow your business. Expand your network by accepting invitations to attend industry parties and functions. Interact with different people; this will help bring new perspectives that will be useful to you. Take note of what you hear on the grapevine; some of this will have great bearing on your plans and next moves for your business. Those of you who have the benefit of advice from a mentor figure should take advice given seriously. For now you can afford to be bold and courageous in your next steps, as luck is currently strongly on your side, but don't make rash decisions. Big success will come to those of you who put enough value on proper planning and strategizing.

LOVE & RELATIONSHIPS - *Settling Down*

Those of you not yet settled will turn your thoughts towards this. Luck in love is good, and if this is what you are looking for, it won't be too difficult to find. If you are already in a relationship, you may be thinking of next steps – getting married, moving in together, starting a family. This is an auspicious time for any of these things, so you can feel confident making plans along this vein.

If you are still very much single, don't play games; if you are serious about someone, let them know or they could well slip right through your fingers. Be bold in your moves; if you are unsure, take the plunge anyway. Things will right themselves and time will help you find a happy balance.

EDUCATION - *New Friendships*

A good month for forging new friendships. You find yourself incredibly popular, so use this time to expand your circle of friends. School is going well and you are full of energy and enthusiasm. Make the best use of this time by keeping a busy schedule; but don't forget to mix in enough play amidst the work. This will keep your mind relaxed and effective.

SECOND MONTH
MARCH 6TH - APRIL 4TH 2015

MISFORTUNE STAR SLOWS YOU DOWN

The coming month sees the *Five Yellow* pay a visit, bringing misfortune luck. Whenever the *wu wang* makes an appearance is when you should be more careful. Pull back on risk-taking, err on the side of caution, and carry or wear the necessary cures. Bad luck comes in a multitude of guises, and the best you can do to reduce its ultimate effect is to reconcile the unbalanced energies of the month. **Wear plenty of gold**. Metal energies will help to keep the afflicted Earth energies under control. Avoid embarking on new initiatives, or scheduling launches or important meetings this month. There may be obstacles that crop up, but don't let these defeat you or get you down. Don't wrack your brains looking for a solution that won't suggest itself. Instead, let things be a while. The problem may even disappear without any interference on your part.

WORK & CAREER - *Stay Low Profile*

Stay low profile in your job. While you need to continue working efficiently, this is not a time when new ideas are well-received. Do not attempt to be too creative. Be a good worker, deliver the results, but avoid adopting a superstar attitude. Steer clear of making big decisions as they are likely to be affected by the negative chi. Delay important judgement calls till later. If you are unhappy about something, you may have to live with it for a while. This is not a time to be complaining about peripheral matters. Fighting small battles and winning them, only to lose the war, will only lead to tears and regrets later. If your situation allows it, this may be a good time to take a holiday. Going on a short vacation will clear your mind and make you more productive when you return.

BUSINESS - *Proceed Cautiously*

You can expect things to be slow when it comes to new business opportunities. Although you won't be short on offers on the table, do proceed cautiously. You may attract some shady characters into your life, and it may not be easy to spot who is and who isn't a fraud. Play it safe by waiting till next month before putting out money or investing in something that carries risk. Grand ideas should be put on hold. There are inauspicious stars in your chart, so this is not the right time to embark on new ventures. Things can easily go wrong. Those active in the stock market should be more careful, since this is a month of loss for you. Even if you think you know what you're doing, it is better to wait for a more opportune time than to jump into something that could get you stuck for some time.

LOVE & RELATIONSHIPS - *Difficult*

Not the best of times when it comes to relationships. With the influence of the *Peach Blossom* as well as the *Five Yellow*, you could well find yourself drawn into a relationship that is not all that good for you. Those of you single should probably put your focus elsewhere this month; avoid entering a new relationship, for things could unravel as quickly as they began... and the aftermath is unlikely to be pretty. Your time now is better spent pursuing other activities. For those of you in relationships, you could find tempers flaring and misunderstandings cropping up for no reason. Back down. There is no need to win every argument. You will find that giving way is the best way of maintaining the peace at this time.

> **FENG SHUI CURE:** Carry the **Heart Sutra Pillar Charm** to nullify the inauspicious energies of the month. The Five Yellow brings all kinds of misfortune; but having the Heart Sutra Pillar near you, the best cure for the *wu wang* this year will help ensure any bad luck that befalls you will be of the sort that does not leave permanent consequences.

THIRD MONTH
APRIL 5TH - MAY 5TH 2015

RELATIONSHIPS TAKE CENTERSTAGE THIS MONTH

The coming month is a month of doubles, when the monthly stars that fly into the various sectors match their host annual stars. What this means for the Dog is a time when relationships take center stage. The number 4 star gets doubled, making this a prolific time for deepening friendships and expanding your circle. In love relationships, passions get heightened, making this a good period for the grand romantic gesture. An auspicious month for engagements, weddings and formalization of vows. The enhanced number 4 star also brings good luck for students and those engaged in learning and research. In work and business, your people skills will give you your edge this month.

WORK & CAREER - *Developing New Skills*

Work will tend to be research-oriented this month, and the more knowledgeable you can make yourself with regards to your particular field of work, the better you will do. Make the effort to improve your current skills and to develop new ones. Investing time in this will contribute a great deal to your career success, especially in the present. This, and making an extra effort to work well in a team situation with your colleagues. You will be buzzing with creative ideas this month, and those of you in lines of work that reward this will do particularly well. You will not always feel this inspired, so while you do, make the most of it to share your ideas and to showcase your originality and ability to think outside the box. For some of you, this will be a turning point month with some exciting new revelations.

BUSINESS - *Networking Pays Off*
Make the most of your ability to get along with others to further your business goals this month. Diligent networking at this time brings tremendous opportunities, sometimes quite unexpected ones. Do not underestimate what a particular someone can do for you. Don't judge a book by its cover; there are treasures under the surface of recently-met acquaintances that will prove distinctly important to you in the near future.

There may be a chance to enter into an exciting joint venture in the coming weeks. If there are any formal agreements to be signed, do so before the month is up. Your luck is good this month, but the luck of benefitting from strategic alliances fades when next month dawns. Boost business luck by carrying the **4/9 Ho Tu mirror amulet.**

LOVE & RELATIONSHIPS - *Blazing Bright*

The energies burn bright for passion, and you feel more ready for romance than you have in a while. Enjoy the time ahead; whether you're looking for fun or for something more serious, the potential is there. This is a good time to come off the singles market, so if there's someone who sparks your interest, pursue the relationship. Don't wait too long or you may miss your chance. For those of you married or in commited relationships, beware of outside temptation. Love is in the air and if there isn't enough of it within your current relationship, there is danger of infidelities.

> **FENG SHUI CURE:** Carry the **Anti-Indifelity Amulet** to keep your marriage or relationship safe against third party interference. The *Peach Blossom* energies of this month bring romance, but sometimes in a dangerous form.

EDUCATION - *Achievement-Oriented*

This is a productive month for the Dog in school. Academically, you are likely to be doing well. You have the potential to achieve top grades and to move right up to the top of the class, as long as you can keep your focus. Believe in yourself because your achievements will only be as high as your goals, so set your sights high.

FOURTH MONTH
MAY 6TH - JUNE 5TH 2015

QUARRELSOME TIME WITH AN EXCESS OF WOOD ENERGY

The exultant energies of the previous month unfortunately come to an abrupt end, and relationships that seemed so sturdy and solid could falter. The number 3 star wreaks havoc in the lives of even the most even-tempered individuals, and for the Dog, the excess of Wood energy the quarrelsome star brings threatens to wear you down. Strengthen yourself with Fire energy – **wear red colours** and **brighten up the Northwest** of your home this month by keeping the lights here turned on. This will help quell the disruptive energies. Keep your temper in check and refrain from reacting on the spot when someone riles you. For some of you, the number 3 brings danger of lawsuits and legal entanglements. Not a good time to fight or to mount any kind of countersuit. Wait till the negative energies blow over.

WORK & CAREER - *Lie Low*

You won't be the easiest person to work with this month, but don't let this wreck relationships you have spent time and effort on building up. Develop a thicker skin. Some of you could find yourselves more sensitive than usual, but try to keep your sense of humour and avoid taking comments and criticism the wrong way. Don't burn bridges by retaliating; you could well be misinterpreting an incident. You are better off moderating the amount of time you spend working directly with others. Not a good time for meetings, discussions or brainstorming. There is some vulnerability to becoming the target of office politics. Lie low and avoid drawing attention to yourself. Carry the **anti-office-politics amulet** or display a **Rooster** on your workdesk.

BUSINESS - *Avoid Risky Ventures*

For Dogs in business, it is better to lie low this month. Do not invest big amounts of money. Avoid risky ventures. Take a vacation and go away for a while even. Your relationships with others tend to be strained, particularly when there are issues involving money. Your fuse is shorter than usual, and this could cause you to be quite unpleasant to deal with. Dog people are usually affable and easy to get along with, but when you get growly, you become quite difficult to take. Your obsession with details could be making you tedious. Avoid making small talk for the sake of it. Keep to the point. Talking for the sake of talking could lead to the wrong things being said.

LOVE & RELATIONSHIPS - *Coming Out Wrong*

This is not the time to impress anyone. Having any expectations at all right now is likely to lead to disappointment, so it is better not to have any. Try and keep things simple in your love relationships. Do not make your partner dwell on your personal miseries with you; you may not like their responses, and you don't need another reason to quarrel. For now, it is better to keep your opinions to yourself. Although you may mean something as a compliment, it may be taken the wrong way. Avoid sensitive subjects and refrain from joking at the expense of others; you don't come across very funny that way, and this could turn others off you.

EDUCATION - *Tow the Line*

Beware of trouble with teachers and authorities. If you are going to break rules, think again. Even if you are doing so to stick up for certain rights you believe in, you could end up being disciplined and suffer for it. Tow the line and suppress your rebellious streak. Focus your pent-up energies on something you can enthusiastic about. The busier the young Dog keeps this month, the better. Don't leave yourself too much time to direct your energies in unhealthy directions.

FIFTH MONTH
JUNE 6TH - JULY 6TH 2015

ILLNESS STAR SAPS YOU OF ENERGY

Your fortunes are clouded by illness energies, so although you may have success in business or at work, you are slowed down somewhat by health concerns. Do not take poor health lightly; a minor ailment could develop into something more serious if you don't look after yourself. On a brighter note, there is promise of money luck this month. You have good opportunities coming your way; how much you can benefit depends on how ambitious you are. Shrug off your insecurities and go after the good things that are within your reach. The month brings success accompanied by personal satisfaction and happiness. Don't let a downbeat attitude stop you from making this a fruitful time.

FENG SHUI CURE: The number 2 star can sap you of energy and also make you more susceptible to catching viruses and falling sick. The **57 year old Earth Dog** and the **45 year old Metal Dog** need to take extra care of themselves. Wear the **Garuda Wu Lou** to counter the illness energies, and do look after yourself this month.

WORK & CAREER - *Schedule Properly*

You enjoy good luck when it comes to career matters, but obstacles arise from poor health and low energy levels. You may feel more tired than usual, so be careful of taking on more than you can manage. Make the effort to schedule properly rather than just winging it; being more organized will let you pace yourself better, something you're likely to need this month. There are good opportunities coming your way, but taking sick days off work or feeling under the weather could see some of these pass you by. Keep your well-being high on your priority list; get enough rest. You will need a clear mind to maximize your opportunities.

BUSINESS - *Rapport Important*

Business luck is good with exciting opportunities in store. Entering a joint venture could lead to something that has long-term potential. The energies of the month favour teaming up, but with the right people. Trust your instincts when it comes to judging potential partners; if something does not feel quite right, pull back. There's great promise if you find partners that you have great rapport with, but if you cannot get along as friends outside of the boardroom, stay wary. Affinity is important for the Dog sign this year. Boost your ally luck by carrying your **Harmony Crest.** You can carry this on your wealth wallet or money clip or in a form that stays close to you at all times. This also helps you attract partners and associates that are honourable and trustworthy, and prepared to stay for the long haul.

LOVE & RELATIONSHIPS - *Supportive*

Those of you married or in steady relationships will find your partner a great source of support. You are luckier as one half of a couple than single, and if you make the effort, you can deepen your bonds with your partner at the intellectual as well as the emotional level. If you are single, you have no problem attracting someone you can see yourself hooking up with; the problem here is that you are unlikely to find the energy to date, unless it happens without too much effort on your part. There is great potential when it comes to romance this month, but you must open your heart up to it.

EDUCATION - *Keeping Focused*

Learning comes easily to the motivated young Dog but because overall your energy levels take a dip, don't try to take on too much. Focusing on doing a few things well will gain you more success than trying to fit in too much. This is a good time to make new friends. You will also find working in study groups productive and good fun. Try it.

SIXTH MONTH
JULY 7TH - AUG 7TH 2015

VICTORY STAR BRINGS PROMISE OF COMPETITIVE SUCCESS

A triumphant time for the Dog, who has the benefit of the *Victory Star* this month. This brings new opportunities and also some changes in your life or lifestyle. There is outstanding success in store for those who know what they want. If you set your heart on something, stay focused and achieving it will not be all that difficult. This is also a lucky time for young student Dogs. Where you need to watch out however has to do with infidelities; there is risk of straying, whether by you or your partner. Protect the NW this month; keep this sector clear of water, as water here exacerbates risk of marriage infidelities. If you value your current relationship, pay more attention to your partner. Leaving each other alone will invite the advances of unwanted outsiders into your union.

FENG SHUI CURE: Carry the **Anti-Infidelity Amulet** this month. The energies bring risk of betrayals of this kind. Don't become a victim of this kind of bad luck.

WORK & CAREER - *Trade-offs*

If you have high ambitions to rise up in your career, this is a time when you should be pursuing those lofty goals of yours. However, to get where you want may involve a major change in lifestyle. This could range from more time on the job, more travel or even an address relocation to another country. If you are prepared to accept the new circumstances that come with the promotion, then things can happen quickly for you. But unfortunately, more likely than not, that will not be the case. If you need to give an answer on a major decision, allow yourself time to think things through before committing. Certainly if your decision involves the family, you should consult with them first.

BUSINESS - *Be Specific*

Those in business can expect a positive month ahead. You have competitive luck on your side, so those of you up against industry rivals will have the benefit of good feng shui winds behind you. This is a good time to promote and differentiate yourself. You enjoy effective leadership luck so put it to good use to galvanize your team. Putting effort into management will see your productivity levels increase. Set yourself clear-cut goals to go after. Don't work without a target. If you want to improve your sales, state by how much. If you want to double profits, give yourself a timeframe. This will focus your mind and increase your discipline so you can achieve more than you thought yourself capable of.

LOVE & RELATIONSHIPS - *New Beginnings*

You're feeling lively and sociable. For some, this could be a turning point in your life. Those of you single could embark on a grand new adventure with someone like-minded. For those of you who have been in a stale relationship for too long, there could be an impending break-up... but not a bitter one. This is the start of a new chapter in your life, a time when change brings benefits, so do not resist it. Embrace it. In fact, look at ways you can do things differently if there are issues in your life you're not happy with. Don't be afraid to let go of the past; once you do, you will see that the future is so much more exciting.

EDUCATION - *Try New Things*

A great month ahead for the student Dog! The Victory Star 1 brings competitive success, making this an ideal time for those of you applying for scholarships, sitting entrance exams, or contributing in class. You are also feeling more lively than usual, allowing you to take on more if you choose. Embark on learning something new, take up a new musical subject, a new instrument, or a new sport.

SEVENTH MONTH
AUG 8TH - SEPT 7TH 2015

DOUBLING OF THE HO TU BRINGS GREAT BENEFITS!

What a wonderful month ahead that brings the promise of great business luck. Finances look good and some of you could experience some kind of windfall. Think longterm when making plans, because your good luck runs into the future. The coming month presents you with great opportunities to build. While you may feel like indulging, and why not, don't just veer off on holiday mode, because when you are feeling this good it is easy to! There is a lot of potential in store for you this month, so keep your eyes and ears open. The *Future Prosperity Star* joins with the number 4 in your chart to double the *Ho Tu* combination of 4/9 that the Dog sign enjoys this Sheep Year. Enhance this auspicious good fortune with the **4/9 Ho Tu mirror** placed in the NW or carried in your bag or pocket.

WORK & CAREER - *Energized*

You find yourself with a ton of energy. Be prepared to shake things up and to suggest new directions if it is your place to do so. Your profile within your work environment gets raised this month and you become firmly entrenched as a core player in the team. This will be quite an honour, and it will also bring new perspectives and new possibilities to your career. This is a time when you could suddenly realize how lucky you are to be doing what you are doing. Your increased input into the strategic side of things will motivate you to even greater heights. You are feeling empowered and energized, and you find it easy to garner support amongst your colleagues and those you associate with. For some of you, monetary gains are also in store. Make the most of your good fortune luck by staying focused, active and on the ball.

BUSINESS - *Many Possibilities*

Growing your workforce and investing in training are good options to consider. It is a beneficial time to focus on building your core team of managers. If you have plans to grow big, identify those who will be helping you bring your ideas to fruition. Remember that as your business grows, you will need more trusted lieutenants. Also, don't forget that what you do and how you plan to do it must make commercial sense. You may have some grand ideas, but if they will not bring the returns, do not waste time pursuing them. You have many avenues of possibilities, but you cannot pursue them all. Make your decisions wisely, then stay resolute in pursuing your chosen goals.

LOVE & RELATIONSHIPS - *Passionate*

The vigorous Fire energy in your chart indicates a hidden passion and adventurism surfacing in your life. If you succumb to your desires, they could either bring you a lot of happiness, or they could cause you endless troubles. Those of you who are single and looking for love will benefit from having a sense of humour. It is this that will attract someone charming into your life. It could well be a case of love at first sight and so it will be something serious. You are unlikely to be interested in flings or relationships where you cannot see a future. Stay single till you find the right one; do not let yourself be pressured into making a commitment you are not ready for. But if you are ready, the future looks very bright indeed!

EDUCATION - *Keeping Busy*

A busy month full of activities both in schoolwork as well as in other activities. There are many things you want to pursue, the only thing stopping you being the number of hours in a day. Do not overcommit or you won't do any one thing well. Choose what you want to pursue for now; you don't need to do everything at once. Save some things for later. But whatever you start now has a chance to make a lasting impact, and could even influence what path your future takes.

EIGHTH MONTH
SEPT 8TH - OCT 7TH 2015

CURRENT PROSPERITY STAR BRINGS MORE LUCKY INDICATIONS YOUR WAY

An auspicious month ahead for the Dog. This is a time when your efforts during the earlier part of the year start to pay off. Things you direct your energies towards bear fruit quickly, and results don't take long in coming. This spurs you onto even greater heights and does wonders for your self-confidence. Use this time to keep yourself busy and to get yourself going. In work and business matters, working with others brings benefits. Opportunities arise for you to work with people you admire. Use the next few weeks to form important new relationships with those you meet on the job. This is also an exciting month for Dogs learning a new skills. When making decisions, trust your instincts, which help you even more than the most careful of analysis. Your mind is working quickly, and the busier you keep yourself, the more efficient you will find you become.

WORK & CAREER - *Enjoyable*
Your confidence gets a boost this month. Others commend your good work and your relationships with those you work with improve substantially. Your

interpersonal skills sharpen up and you will find it easy to get along with others. You are likely to be given more responsibilities and you will relish being depended on. You will find what you are doing more enjoyable than ever. Your talent and dependability become obvious to others, but this happily does not stir up envy; instead, others want you on their side. There is money luck for those of you earning on commission. There is also the promise of promotion. While this may not come immediately, it is something to work towards, and if you are contributing in a valuable way to the company, it will not go unnoticed.

BUSINESS - *Opportunities*

Your wealth luck is ripening and those in business find many goldmines to tap if you keep your eyes open. You can afford to be daring in your decisions. If you feel something is worth pursuing, this is the time to go for it. Those of you considering going into business with another party can do so assuredly; things started now tend to work out well for the Dog. Be decisive when making decisions, and don't waver once you've made your choices. You make a good leader and boss as long as you don't let your insecurities surface. Avoid people or situations that make you lose confidence. This year, as long as you can suppress your tendency to feel insecure about your abilities, you can achieve a lot. You have good luck, but your weak element indications may convince you otherwise. Don't let them.

LOVE & RELATIONSHIPS - *Promising*

Your key to happiness in love lies in good communication. Share what's on your mind. If you need to say something, go ahead. Don't keep feelings bottled up or this can lead to misunderstandings. Problems within your relationship will only materialize if you let them. You enjoy the influence of the *Peach Blossom Star*, and this month you are further blessed by the *Star of Current Prosperity*. For those who are married, pursuing hobbies and shared interests with your spouse will draw the two of you even closer to one another. Those of you at the dating stage will see the pace of your relationship pick up, and move to the next level of commitment.

EDUCATION - *Scholastic Luck*

Your ambitions are riding high and you have a self-assurance that could make you come across brash or boastful. Academically, this is a good time for the young Dog. Study comes easily and you may well find some topics too easy. Go with the flow but there is no need to become a show-off or you could put some people off. Play nice and enjoy this period, when your confidence gets a happy boost.

NINTH MONTH
OCT 8TH - NOV 6TH 2015

AFFLICTED ENERGIES THIS MONTH.
RISK OF LOSS, BETRAYAL. BE CAREFUL

The number 7 star brings risk of robbery, violence and money loss. This is a strongly afflictive star, which you should make every effort to suppress. Because it makes an appearance in your chart, do carry the **Anti-Robbery Amulet**, which deflects its harmful energies. Donate some money to charity; this will help reduce the negative impact of the #7 on you. It is a month to be more cautious when out and about, and to take security and personal safety more seriously. There is risk of betrayal by those you trust, particularly when it comes to money. Be wary of new acquaintances that make an appearance in your life at this juncture; they may not be good news. Avoid taking risks. Not a good month to invest, speculate, gamble or expand. Keep a low profile and let the afflictive energies pass.

WORK & CAREER - *Office Politics*

You can expect some aggravations at work. Just when you are getting comfortable, an obstacle or problem crops up. Take these in your stride and don't let them get you riled up. The calmer you can keep, the better you can solve whatever issue you get faced with. Unfortunately your colleagues are not of all that much help right now. Beware office politics; even those you consider your friends could let you down in this way. Stay close to the boss and keep on top of everything. The Dog is usually a straightforward and highly ethical character – and playing someone else out to get ahead is not in your blood at all – so when someone does that to you it could come as a shock. Be aware of everything that's going on around you. You don't have to play dirty, but you can be smart so you don't fall victim to someone else's game.

FENG SHUI TIP: At work the **Anti-Office Politics Amulet** will help keep you out of the line of fire of harmful politicking at the workplace. Be shrewd in your conduct and in your reading of others. Don't reveal too much. Keep your personal life to yourself. Not a good month to become overly close to those you work with.

BUSINESS - *Pay Attention*

Dogs in business will need to use their cleverness to stay ahead of the competition. There is risk of being cheated, so try not to let anything slip by you. Be extra vigilant to the goings-on within your company. Keep a tight rein on the finances. If something looks amiss, investigate further. This is a time when paying attention to details will pay off. Misunderstandings with others may arise due to the negative combination of stars. If you have other partners in your business, keep everyone informed of decisions made or you may find a lawsuit on your hands. Think of long-term consequences before doing anything to jeopardize a good partnership arrangement.

LOVE & RELATIONSHIPS - *Drama*

There could well be high drama when it comes to your love life this month. The *Peach Blossom* star in your chart gets stirred up, and instead of bringing romance, it could bring headaches and worries. Don't let outsiders stir things up between you and your partner. Because you tend to be more on edge than usual, it is easy for others to interfere. Remember where your loyalties should lie. For some of you, there could be temptation. While you may think yourself the faithful kind, anything can happen. Don't let a bad one-off decision spoil things for you.

The single Dog is not immune to the hazards of the month's sharp energies; dating becomes complicated when you are seeing more than one person. Even if you are not formally an item with any particular person. Be sensitive to such issues, or you could incite jealousies that can turn into violence.

TENTH MONTH
NOV 7TH - DEC 6TH 2015

HEAVEN STAR BRINGS NEW OPPORTUNITIES & SUCCESS LUCK

The number 6 flies in to join the number 4, bringing you *sum-of-ten* completion luck. Plans put into motion earlier can come to a successful close. In business, profitable deals can be made. Investment luck is promising. Results come quickly. This is a time when you have the helping hand of heaven showing you the way, making your instincts sharp and bringing new opportunities to your notice. Things fall nicely into place. Young Dogs – in school or starting out in their careers – have excellent *mentor luck*, with someone helping them whether in an advisory capacity or by opening doors. Make the most of this auspicious time by staying active, seizing opportunities and working hard.

WORK & CAREER - *Big Decisions*

Your mind is clear and you are thinking on your feet. This makes it easy for you to do your job well and to enjoy it at the same time. There are exciting developments on the horizon, with the potential of upward mobility in your career. Your hard work show results and you will be offered more challenging assignments to handle. You know instinctively if something is going right. Relationship luck is good, so your success is unlikely to lead to jealousy. Some of you could be facing some big decisions career-wise. Before making big choices, think things through carefully. However, if you feel something is right, go with your instincts. There's no looking back once you make up your mind but rest assured luck is on your side for things to turn out well for you, whatever you choose.

BUSINESS - *Big Luck*

The Dog in business can look forward to a wonderful month ahead. New initiatives pursued at this time will turn out well. Use the advice of friends and mentors in the know. Stay alert to new opportunities coming your way. You may need some help to get things started; don't hesitate to ask, there are many looking for the right opportunity to work with you or to get to know you better. You are feeling positive and your buoyant mood rubs off on those you work with. Generate enthusiasm within your team. Boost your own confidence by mixing with people who bring out the best in you. Don't let yourself be talked out of pursuing what you want to do; trust your own instincts. Think big. You have this kind of luck right now, but you can only capture it if you believe in it then go after it.

LOVE & RELATIONSHIPS - *Enjoyable*

You will find socializing and making new friends
something you enjoy immensely this month. You have
a very positive aura and others seek out your company.
You are open to ideas and this makes you wonderfully
enjoyable to spend time with. Those of you single and
available could well find someone special to set your
sights on. Be bold with your feelings; no one can resist a
confident Dog person. Those who are married can make
your spouse very happy this month! This is an auspicious
time all around, and a good one for getting married,
starting or expanding a family, and making plans for the
future.

EDUCATION - *Set Specific Goals*

The Dog in school benefits from taking your cue from
someone you can mentor. You are feeling energetic and
achievment-oriented, and if someone who cares about
you takes an interest in what you are doing, you will do
even better! Your attitude is wonderful and if you are
working on specific goals, they become easy to achieve.
Don't sail through the days aimlessly. Making detailed
plans will help you stay focused. While plans can always
change, it is still important to have them. By all means
be flexible, but be focused.

ELEVENTH MONTH
DEC 7TH 2015 - JAN 5TH 2016

MISFORTUNE STAR MANIFESTS TEMPORARY OBSTACLES TO HURDLE

Your chart this month indicates misfortune and loss, so this is a time to be defensive rather than aggressive. The misfortune star threatens to wreak havoc in your life, so to escape serious adversity, it is important for you to carry the **Heart Sutra Pillar**. You should also place one in the Northwest of your home and office. This is the best way to keep the afflicted energies of the month under control. Avoid taking risks in your work, in business and also against accidents and injury. If you are involved in dangerous sports, refrain from these activities this month. You may face obstacles and stressful situations, but use them to strengthen your character. This could be one of those times when you need to call on your inner strength to help you through, but whatever glitches you face are only temporary unless you let them defeat you.

WORK & CAREER - *Lie Low*

This is a time to watch your back! When the energies are as fierce as they are, even friends can become temporary foes. There will be challenges to face, and sometimes it may be tempting to act on impulse and throw in the towel. But before making any brash decisions, calm your mind and think things through. Things will not stay difficult. The energies improve when the *wu wang* moves out of your chart, but while it is here, you will need to learn to dodge its afflictive chi. Some of you will face fierce competition at the workplace. Vying for the boss' approval can become exhausting, and the best way around this may be to lie low and let others have their glory. You can make up for lost time next month when your luck improves. But setting your sights too high now could cause your downfall. Not the time to "peak".

BUSINESS - *New Approaches*

Things may feel like they have come to a standstill. Projects that seemed to be moving along fine could suddenly face obstacles. Don't let temporary difficulties floor you. Perhaps a new approach is needed. Take time to think things through. While you may have to change course, don't abandon your goals. The Five Yellow can be challenging, but sometimes challenges are just what you need to realign your perspectives. Be sure however to have your Five Yellow cures in place, because what you don't want is for serious misfortune to befall you. Don't put yourself at risk, financially or otherwise. Err on the side of caution whenever making decisions this month.

Plan to roll out new initiatives after the month is over. Not a good time to hire new people or to expand the team. But you can work on improving the camaraderie between you and those you already work with.

LOVE & RELATIONSHIPS - *Unexciting*
Luck in love takes a dip. Your love life is unlikely to be very exciting, but you are also not particularly in the mood for romance. You have other things on your mind, and forcing yourself to make small talk is not something that tickles your fancy right now. You have a short fuse, which does not endear you to others much. Unless you find someone who can tolerate your current eccentricities, this is not the most opportune time to hook up.

EDUCATION - *Keep Striving*
Things may not go according to plan, and you may start to feel insecure for whatever reason. Don't let one or two bad experiences deter you. Keep striving to do well in your studies. Temporary setbacks will not last into the long term, and they can be overcome as long as you have the right attitude. You are as clever as the next person, and there is no need to be a "natural" at whatever you are trying to learn. But a lot of your potential can only show through if you believe in yourself.

TWELFTH MONTH
JAN 6TH - FEB 3RD 2016

DOUBLE PEACH BLOSSOM FIRES UP THE ROMANCE!

The energies of the month are intense, with the double 4 bringing love and romance to the fore. You are feeling sociable and in need of attention, and you are happiest this month when surrounded by people, especially by those who adore you. You have no problem being the center of attention, and this month you in fact crave it. You are done playing the underdog, and now you seek out opportunities to shine. Go for it because luck is with you! You enjoy good relationships with others, who warm towards your enthusiastic attitude. In your career, make efforts to showcase your skills. There is no need to be overly self-deprecating. When success starts manifesting, there could be some jealousy to contend with, but nothing you cannot handle.

WORK & CAREER - *Productive*

The workplace is a playground for the Dog! You are feeling confident and energetic, and the more you have on your plate, the happier you will be. You get along well with others and you also make a terrific team player. You have good ideas to share, and the alliances you have forged over the past year will pay off. You could catch the eye of the boss and there is some promotion luck within reach. You have a lot of good ideas up your sleeve; continue to share them. You are feeling creative, and your work is likely to bring you not just success, but also personal satisfaction.

BUSINESS - *New Possibilities*

Success this month stems from your great skill with people. Relationships you have spent time nurturing over the year become invaluable now, with various acquaintances and elements fitting together nicely like a jigsaw, bringing together new possibilities and great promise for the future. There are some truly exciting projects to sink your teeth in, and while the rewards may not come overnight, you have a clear plan.

You are financially in a good position, and even if you need a cash injection, you have no trouble raising the funds if you have a proper plan in place. It will be just as much if not more about who you know, as well as what you know, so don't neglect this aspect of your strategy. Be bold and be a good leader. Those who work under you look up to you, so the more strength you can give them with your confidence, the greater your prospects become. A particularly

LOVE & RELATIONSHIPS - *Centrestage*

Those of you still single could find love and romance taking centre stage. There could well already be someone you've set your sights on, and even if you don't, someone is likely to come along to really sweep you off your feet. Enjoy the ride. Let yourself be whimsical and romantic. Those already in steady relationships will find yourselves experiencing new levels of intimacy with your partner. It may have been some time since you've made such a connection with anybody. Let yourself experience the whole works. There is no need to be guarded when it comes to love, the energies are auspicious and there is a lot of happiness in store. Do watch out however that you do not get yourself entangled in an illicit love affair, as that could be much more trouble than it is worth, and could lead to great unhappiness. Protect against the flip-side of the *Peach Blossom* wielding its influence by carrying or wearing the **Anti-Infidelity Amulet**.

EDUCATION - *Superlative*

The stars this month especially favour the young Dog. A double dose of the number 4 star brings enormous good fortune in learning and research; those of you expanding your knowledge will find it easier to stay focused, with some revelations that make the whole process easier and more enjoyable.

for more on all the recommended
feng shui cures, remedies & enhancers for

2015
please log on to

www.fsmegamall.com/2015